The Word and the Spirit

Rev. C. H. Spurgeon

Ten sermons on the theme of the Word of God and the work of the Holy Spirit

The New Park Street Pulpit and The Metropolitan Tabernacle Pulpit

EP EVANGELICAL PRESS

EVANGELICAL PRESS
Faverdale North Industrial Estate, Darlington, DL3 0PH, England

Evangelical Press USA
P. O. Box 825, Webster, New York 14580, USA

e-mail: sales@evangelicalpress.org

web: http://www.evangelicalpress.org

First published 2005

British Library Cataloguing in Publication Data available

ISBN 0 85234 5453

Printed and bound in Great Britain by Creative Print and Design Wales, Ebbw Vale, South Wales.

Contents

Foreword

C. H. Spurgeon (1834-1892) and his teaching on the Holy Spirit[1]

Charles Haddon Spurgeon was born into a godly home in the heart of rural Essex on 19 June 1834. Spurgeon's forebears originally came from the Netherlands, which they had left in the sixteenth century due to religious persecution. Both Spurgeon's father, John Spurgeon (1811-1902), and his grandfather, James Spurgeon (1776-1864), were Congregationalist preachers, and it was during an extended stay over a number of years in the home of his grandfather that Spurgeon was first exposed to the writings of the Puritans. James Spurgeon was the pastor of the Congregational church in the village of Stambourne in the heart of rural Essex. Here in the parsonage the young Spurgeon discovered a library of Puritan folios. They had been collected by Henry Havers (1620-c.1712), who had pastored the Stambourne church after his ejection from the Church of England in 1662 when he refused to comply with the Act of Uniformity.

Despite Spurgeon's tender years and the fact that as a young child he found it very difficult to lift these large and weighty Puritan volumes, he would later write that as a boy he was never happier than when in the company of these Puritan authors.[2] After his conversion in January 1850, Spurgeon collected original Puritan editions with zest and fervour. Not content with reading the works of these seventeenth-century authors himself, he never ceased to recommend them to his fellow believers. For instance, in a sermon entitled 'Paul — his cloak and his books', which Spurgeon preached in November 1863, he urged his hearers to follow the apostle Paul's example and to read good books: 'Renounce as much as you will all light literature, but study as much as possible sound theological works, especially the Puritanic writers, and expositions of the Bible. We are quite persuaded that the very best way for you to be spending your leisure is to be either reading or praying.'[3]

Spurgeon was especially convinced that wide exposure to the Puritans was a vital part of ministerial training. Thus, at his Pastors' College, which was founded in 1856, the theology that was taught was rooted in the Puritans. In defence of this methodology, Spurgeon said, 'We are old-fashioned enough to prefer Manton to Maurice, Charnock to Robertson, and Owen to Voysey. Both our experience and our reading of the Scriptures confirm us in the belief of the unfashionable doctrines of grace; and among us, upon those grand fundamentals, there is no uncertain sound.'[4]

Indeed, Spurgeon was rightly convinced that it was commitment to these doctrines that had preserved the Baptist denomination over the centuries.[5]

Spurgeon — heir of the Puritan interest in the Holy Spirit

Now, one of the distinctive marks of Puritan theology is its emphasis on the person and work of the Holy Spirit. Numerous authors over the years have commented on this distinct characteristic. B. B. Warfield (d. 1921), Spurgeon's younger contemporary, noted eight years after Spurgeon's death that 'The developed doctrine of the work of the Holy Spirit is an exclusively Reformation doctrine, and more particularly a Reformed doctrine, and more particularly still a Puritan doctrine... Puritan thought was almost entirely occupied with loving study of the work of the Holy Spirit, and found its highest expression in dogmatico-practical expositions of the several aspects of it.'[6]

More recently, Richard F. Lovelace has reiterated Warfield's judgement and maintained that 'The English Puritans (particularly John Owen and Richard Sibbes) have given us the most profound and extensive biblical-theological studies of the ministry of the Holy Spirit which exist in any language.'[7] Given Spurgeon's love for, and constant study of, the Puritans, it is not at all surprising that this leading characteristic of Puritanism is also reproduced in Spurgeon's sermons and writings. In fact, so extensive is the material by Spurgeon on the person and work of the Spirit that it would take a monograph devoted to the subject to do real justice to his teaching on the Holy Spirit. What follows, though, has a much more modest goal, namely, to provide an introduction to the Baptist preacher's doctrine of the Holy Spirit by focusing on his conviction that 'Where the Spirit of God is, there is power.'[8]

The vital necessity of the Holy Spirit

During 1859, when a powerful revival swept through much of Great Britain, Spurgeon preached a series of sermons on what are sometimes referred to as 'the five points of Calvinism'. He was firmly convinced that the proclamation of these doctrines would help further the revival that was then underway.[9] One of these sermons, entitled 'The necessity of the Spirit's work', begins by sketching the biblical teaching on men and women outside of Christ: they are dead in sin, 'utterly and entirely averse to everything that is good and right', totally unwilling to come to Christ.[10] Only the Spirit, Spurgeon avers, can remedy this situation; he alone can change the will, 'correct the bias of the heart', set men and women on the right road and 'give [them] strength to run in it'.[11]

When Spurgeon turns to examine the means by which the Spirit brings men and women to Christ — for instance, the preaching of the Word — and the means by which he takes them on to maturity — for example, baptism and the Lord's Supper — he finds that all of these means are completely inadequate unless the Spirit deigns to use them.[12] Indeed, Spurgeon stresses, until the Spirit calls the unbeliever out of darkness into the light of God's kingdom, his or her 'election is a dead letter'.[13]

Likewise, the redemption accomplished by the Lord Jesus is of no avail, until the Spirit applies Christ's redemptive work to the soul: 'Christ's blood and righteousness are like wine stored in the wine-vat; but we cannot get thereat. The Holy Spirit dips our vessel into this precious wine, and then we drink; but without the Spirit we must die and perish just as much, though the Father elect and the Son redeem, as though the Father had never elected, and though the Son had never bought us with his blood. The Spirit is absolutely necessary. Without him neither the works of the Father, nor of the Son, are of any avail to us.'[14]

Spurgeon concludes this sermon by stressing that the vital necessity of the Spirit's work in the believer does not come to an end at conversion, for 'The acceptable acts of the Christian's life cannot be performed without the Spirit.'[15] Four years later, preaching on Acts 2:1-4, Spurgeon again emphasized 'How absolutely necessary is the presence and power of the Holy Spirit.' He said, 'It is not possible for us to promote the glory of God or to bless the souls of men, unless the Holy Ghost shall be in us and with us. Those who were assembled on that memorable day of Pentecost were all men of prayer and faith, but even these precious gifts are only available when the celestial fire sets them on a blaze… [Even] these favoured and honoured saints can do nothing without the breath of God the Holy Ghost… [If] so it was with them, much more must it be the case with us. Let us beware of trusting to our well-adjusted machineries of committees and schemes; let us be jealous of all reliance upon our own mental faculties or religious vigour; let us be careful that we do not look too much to our leading preachers and evangelists, for if we put any of these in the place of the divine Spirit, we shall err most fatally.'[16]

This absolute need of the Spirit on the part of the church and of the individual believer is a constant refrain in Spurgeon's sermons and writings over the next twenty-nine years till his death in 1892. For instance, in a sermon preached in 1864 on 'The superlative excellence of the Holy Spirit', he challenges his hearers: 'Do not say that we want money; we shall have it soon enough when the Spirit touches men's hearts. Do not say that we want buildings, churches, edifices; all these may be very well in subserviency, but the main want of the church is the Spirit, and men into whom the Spirit may be poured.'[17]

Thus, Spurgeon was constrained to pray in the middle of the sermon: 'Come, Holy Spirit, come, we can do nothing without thee, but if we have thy wind, we spread our sail, and speed onward towards glory.'[18]

Keeping in step with the Spirit

The church's need of the Spirit carries with it certain responsibilities, and Spurgeon, like his beloved Puritans, was not slow to point these out. In 'The superlative excellence of the Holy Spirit', Spurgeon emphasizes that the Spirit must be treated with 'deep awe and reverence'. Believers must be careful not to grieve him or, through sin, provoke him to anger. Moreover, if 'The Holy Spirit be indeed so mighty, let us do nothing without him; let us begin no project, and carry on no enterprise, and conclude no transaction, without imploring his blessing.'[19]

In a later sermon, entitled 'The Paraclete', which was preached in 1872, Spurgeon reminded his audience that if they truly considered the Spirit to be their 'sole force', then they ought to 'Love the Spirit, worship the Spirit, trust the Spirit, obey the Spirit, and, as a church, cry mightily to the Spirit. Beseech him to let his mighty power be known and felt among you.'[20] And putting his own advice into practice, Spurgeon went on to cry: 'Come, Holy Spirit, now! Thou art with us, but come with power and let us feel thy sacred might!'[21]

Spurgeon was all too aware of the consequences of failing to heed such advice. In a sermon preached two years before 'The Paraclete', the Baptist preacher laid before the congregation of the Metropolitan Tabernacle what he called 'A most needful prayer concerning the Holy Spirit'. His text was the prayer of David in Psalm 51:11: 'Cast me not away from thy presence; and take not thy Holy Spirit from me' (AV). After a personal confession, in which Spurgeon declared that he 'would sooner die a thousand times, than lose the helpful presence of the Holy Ghost', he used a vivid illustration, fresh in the minds of his hearers, to depict the church from which the Spirit has departed. On the other side of the English Channel the Franco-Prussian War was raging, and, as Spurgeon preached, the war was going badly for the French, who would suffer a humiliating defeat at the hands of the Prussians at the end of that year. 'Any church from which the Spirit has departed', Spurgeon declared, 'becomes very like that great empire with whose military glory the world was dazzled, and whose strength made the nations tremble. France, mistress of arms, queen of beauty, arbiter of politics, how soon has she fallen! ... The nation once so great now lies bleeding at her victor's feet, pitied of us all none the less because her folly continues the useless fight. Just so have we seen it in churches; may we never so see it here.'[22]

Spurgeon turns to the geography of Egypt to drive his point home even further. Areas of land in Egypt which were once fertile because of life-giving irrigation canals drawn from the Nile River are now desert simply because these canals have been allowed to lapse into disuse. So it is with churches, Spurgeon emphasizes. Churches 'irrigated by the Spirit', he declared, 'once produced rich harvests of souls; left of the Spirit the sand of the world has covered them, and where once all was green and beautiful there is nothing but the former howling wilderness.'[23]

Sticking with Egypt for a further illustration, Spurgeon takes up an aspect of the history of that land. The nineteenth century witnessed the systematic ransacking of the Egyptian pyramids by European archaeologists and explorers. Prominent among the treasures found in these pyramids were the mummified bodies of the Pharaohs. Spurgeon clearly has little sympathy with the removal of these bodies of the ancient Egyptian kings. Their discovery and exposure to 'every vulgar eye' awakens in Spurgeon 'melancholy reflections'. What was 'once a Pharaoh whose voice could shake a nation and devastate continents' is now a mere object for a museum.

And now Spurgeon draws the comparison with the local church: '... alive by the divine indwelling, God gives it royalty, and makes it a king and priest unto himself among the sons of men; its influence is felt further than it dreams; the world trembles at it, for it is fair as the sun, clear as the moon, and terrible as an army with banners; but when the Spirit of God is departed, what remains but its old records, ancient creeds, title-deeds, traditions, histories and memories? It is in fact a mummy of a church rather than a church of God, and it is better fitted to be looked at by antiquarians than to be treated as an existent agency.'[24]

The Holy Spirit and the pastor

Spurgeon was also insistent that those who pastor and preach should be continually conscious of their deep need of the Spirit of God. At his Pastors' College he particularly sought to inculcate such a consciousness in the minds and hearts of the students. The college had begun in 1856 with one student, Thomas W. Medhurst (1834-1917). By 1877, there were 110 men attending the college full-time.[25] That same year Spurgeon published his *Second Series of Lectures to My Students*, a series of addresses that he had regularly given at the college on Friday afternoons. In the first volume of lectures, which he admitted were more akin to sermons than lectures, Spurgeon had explored the pastor's life as it relates to his walk with God, his preaching, and his health. In this second book Spurgeon treated, among other things, the pastor's relationship to the Holy Spirit.

After some initial remarks on the reality of the Spirit's existence, Spurgeon comes to what he describes in no uncertain terms as 'the core of our subject'. For those who are ministers, he solemnly declares: '… the Holy Spirit is absolutely essential. Without him our office is a mere name. We claim no priesthood over and above that which belongs to every child of God, but we are the successors of those who, in olden times, were moved of God to declare his word, to testify against transgression, and to lead his cause. Unless we have the spirit of the prophets resting upon us, the mantle which we wear is nothing but a rough garment to deceive. We ought to be driven forth with abhorrence from the society of honest men for daring to speak in the name of the Lord if the Spirit of God rests not upon us.'[26]

In what areas, Spurgeon goes on to ask, should those in pastoral ministry especially seek the help of the Spirit? Spurgeon proceeds to answer this question with a list of several areas in which the Spirit's aid is vital. Quoting John 16:13, a favourite passage of his when it came to discussing the work of the Spirit, Spurgeon states that the Spirit is the 'Spirit of *knowledge*'. He opens up the Scriptures, and takes especial delight in focusing the pastor's attention on 'the centre of our testimony', the person and work of the Lord Jesus.[27]

The Spirit is also the 'Spirit of *wisdom*', the one who gives the ability to rightly apply the knowledge obtained from the study of Scripture and to preach with balance. For instance, Spurgeon is convinced that '… many brethren who preach human responsibility deliver themselves in so legal a manner as to disgust all those who love the doctrines of grace. On the other hand, I fear that many have preached the sovereignty of God in such a way as to drive all persons who believe in man's free agency entirely away from the Calvinistic side. We should not hide truth for a moment, but we should have wisdom so to preach it that there shall be no needless jarring or offending.'[28]

Then the Spirit is needed to give *fluency of speech* and *freedom in preaching*. Comparing the Spirit to the live coal from the altar in the vision of the prophet Isaiah (Isa. 6:6), Spurgeon states, 'Oh, how gloriously a man speaks when his lips are blistered with the live coal from the altar — feeling the burning power of the truth, not only in his inmost soul, but on the very lip with which he is speaking!'[29]

The Spirit's fourth aid in preaching is as 'an *anointing oil*' on the preacher as he preaches, that is, enabling his mind and heart to be wrapped up in the subject of the sermon.[30] In a sermon that Spurgeon preached on Hag. 2:4-5 in September 1886, the London Baptist made a similar point: 'Oh, that the prayers of God's people would always go up for God's ministers, that they may speak with a divine power and influence which none shall be able to gainsay! We look too much for clever men; we seek out fluent and flowery speakers; we sigh for men cultured and trained in all the knowledge of the heathen: nay, but if we sought more for unction, for divine authority, and for that power which doth hedge about the man of God, how much wiser should we be! Oh, that all of us who profess to preach the gospel would learn to speak in entire dependence upon the direction of the Holy Spirit, not daring to utter our own words, but even trembling lest we should do so, and committing ourselves to that secret influence without which nothing will be powerful upon the conscience or converting to the heart. Know ye not the difference between the power that cometh of human oratory, and that which cometh by the divine energy which speaks so to the heart that men cannot resist it? We have forgotten this too much. It were better to speak six words in the power of the Holy Ghost than to preach seventy years of sermons without the Spirit. He who rested on those who have gone to their reward in heaven can rest this day upon ministers and bless our evangelists, if we will but seek it of him. Let us cease to grieve the Spirit of God, and look to him for help to the faithful ministers who are yet spared to us.'[31]

A final way in which the Spirit helps in preaching is to *produce effects* in those who listen: 'Miracles of grace must be the seals of our ministry; who can bestow them but the Spirit of God? Convert a soul without the Spirit of God! Why, you cannot even make a fly, much less create a new heart and a right spirit... Therefore, with strong crying and tears, wait upon him from day to day.'[32]

Little wonder, Spurgeon comments, that the root cause of many useless ministries lies in the 'lack of distinctly recognizing the power of the Holy Ghost'.[33]

Remarkable instances

A remarkable illustration of Spurgeon's own dependence upon the Spirit in the pulpit occurs in his autobiography. Discussing instances of striking conversions under his preaching ministry, he relates that on one occasion he deliberately pointed to a man in the congregation and said: '"There is a man sitting there, who is a shoemaker; he keeps his shop open on Sundays, it was open last Lord's Day morning, he took ninepence, and there was fourpence profit out of it; his soul is sold to Satan for fourpence!" A city missionary, when going his rounds, met with this man, and seeing that he was reading one of my sermons, he asked the question, "Do you know Mr Spurgeon?" "Yes," replied the man, "I have every reason to know him, I have been to hear him, and, under his preaching, by God's grace I have become a new creature in Christ Jesus. Shall I tell you how it happened? I went to the Music Hall, and took my seat in the middle of the place. Mr Spurgeon looked at me as if he knew me, and in his sermon he pointed to me, and told the congregation that I was a shoemaker, and that I kept my shop open on Sundays, and I did, sir. I should not have minded that, but he also said that I took ninepence the Sunday before, and there was fourpence profit out of it. I did take ninepence that day, and fourpence was just the profit, but how he should know that, I could not tell. Then it struck me that it was God who had spoken to my soul through him, so I shut up my shop the next Sunday. At first, I was afraid to go again to hear him, lest he should tell the people more about me, but afterwards I went, and the Lord met with me, and saved my soul."'[34]

Spurgeon went on to say that there were as 'many as a dozen similar cases' in which he 'pointed at somebody in the hall without having the slightest knowledge of the person, or any idea that what I said was right, except that I believed I was moved by the Spirit to say it; and so striking has been my description, that the persons have gone away, and said to their friends, "Come, see a man that told me all things that ever I did; beyond a doubt, he must have been sent of God to my soul, or else he could not have described me so exactly."'[35]

Now, what is so significant about these extraordinary instances in the life of Spurgeon is that he did not make a 'ministry' out of them, as some would do today. They were obviously out of the norm, but Spurgeon mentions them primarily to exalt the grace of God in the salvation of sinners.

Further on the Holy Spirit and the pastor

The work of the ministry, though, contains more than preaching and its preparation in the study. There is also the important matter of prayer. Central to the minister's life is 'praying in the Holy Spirit', and Spurgeon rightly advises, 'That minister who does not think so had better escape from his ministry.'[36] But to maintain this life of communion with God the minister needs 'secret oil to be poured upon the sacred fire of [his] heart's devotion'; he wants 'again and again [to be] visited by the Spirit of grace and supplications' (Zech. 12:10).[37] Then, the minister also needs the Spirit to walk in holiness in every area of his life and to keep himself 'unspotted from the world'.[38] Finally, those in pastoral ministry have much need of discernment in their dealings with men and women, and here again the Spirit is absolutely necessary, 'For he knows the minds of men as he knows the mind of God.'[39]

Spurgeon was well aware that this list of ways in which the pastor needs the Spirit's help is far from complete, but evidently his time was running out, and he wanted to remind his listeners (and later, his readers) that the Spirit's necessary assistance may be lost: '... it is certain that ministers may lose the aid of the Holy Ghost... You shall not perish as believers, for everlasting life is in you, but you may perish as ministers, and be no more heard of as witnesses for the Lord.'[40]

If this happens, there is surely a reason. Spurgeon gives a list of reasons, ranging from disobedience to the Spirit's promptings to neglect of private prayer. A gallery of individuals from Scripture who experienced the withdrawal of the Spirit's power then follows: some, like Balaam, were sons of perdition; others, like Samson, were children of God. In the light of these examples, Spurgeon can only pray for himself, his hearers and his readers: 'Oh, for the Spirit of God to make and keep us alive unto God, faithful to our office, and useful to our generation, and clear of the blood of men's souls.'[41]

The greatest fight in the world

One of the main ways that Spurgeon kept in touch with graduates of the Pastors' College was through the College Conference. First held for five days in March 1865, it was soon shifted to the month of September. An eagerly anticipated occasion, the annual conference helped to revive the flagging spirits of many of the graduates who laboured in difficult circumstances in remote areas of the country or in urban areas hardened against the gospel and dangerous to health. The late 1880s, however, saw the disruption of this conference as Spurgeon sought to repel what he rightly saw as the encroachment of liberal theology on English Baptist churches. A good number of the graduates of his college, though, failed to take his side in what came to be called the 'Down-Grade controversy'. The annual conference was consequently re-formed and from 1888 on this re-formed conference met in the month of April.[42]

The theme of the conference in 1891, the last one that Spurgeon ever attended, was the work of the Spirit.[43] As the president of the Pastors' College, Spurgeon gave what was his customary presidential address on the morning of Tuesday, 21 April. This address, which took close to an hour and a half to deliver, was later published as *The Greatest Fight in the World* and was considered by Spurgeon as a concise declaration of his position vis-à-vis the Down-Grade controversy.

The address is divided into three parts: our armoury, namely, the Word of God; our army, namely, the church of God; and our strength, namely, the Spirit of God. Nearly half of the talk is devoted to a defence of God's Word as infallible and perfect, a reflection of the fact that among the central issues of the Down-Grade controversy was the nature of Scripture.

When Spurgeon comes to the final part of the address, he begins by highlighting the fact that the pastor's dependence upon the Spirit must be a practical reality, and not merely something theoretical. For instance, having read *The Gospel Worthy of All Acceptation* by the Calvinistic Baptist Andrew Fuller (1754-1815), or *A Discourse Concerning the Holy Spirit* by the Puritan divine John Owen (1616-1683), does not mean that one knows the truths which the authors discuss in these books. 'We know nothing,' Spurgeon maintains, 'till we are taught by the Holy Ghost, who speaks to the heart.'[44] Spurgeon then details a few areas in which the pastor must depend upon the Spirit, all of which would have been familiar territory to graduates of the Pastors' College who had heard Spurgeon's Friday afternoon lectures.

From the work of the Spirit Spurgeon turns to the pastor's experience of the Spirit and he gives his audience the timeless reminder that 'When the Spirit of God is gone, even truth itself becomes an iceberg.'[45] A few remarks on how best to secure the Spirit's help then follow. In this regard, Spurgeon especially urges his hearers never to consider the Holy Spirit as anything less than a fully divine person: 'Worship him [that is, the Spirit] as the adorable Lord God. Never call the Holy Spirit "it"; nor speak of him as if he were a doctrine, or an influence, or an orthodox myth. Reverence him, love him, and trust him with familiar yet reverent confidence. He is God; let him be God to you.'[46]

Behind this statement is Spurgeon's concern that there was a slippage in English Baptist circles regarding the personhood of the Holy Spirit. Four years earlier, as noted above, at the beginning of the Down-Grade controversy, Spurgeon had outlined a number of areas which he considered to be threatened by the inroads of liberal theology: 'The atonement is scouted, the inspiration of Scripture is derided, the Holy Spirit is degraded into an influence, the punishment of sin is turned into fiction, and the resurrection into a myth.'[47]

While controversy over the personhood of the Spirit was not a prominent aspect of the Down-Grade controversy, Spurgeon was well aware that acceptance of the other key tenets of liberal theology invariably led to a rejection of this precious biblical truth.[48] He would no doubt have appreciated the recent warning of Peter Berger, a Christian social scientist: 'He who sups with the devil of modernity had better have a long spoon.'[49] Firmly attached to the personhood of the Spirit from the earliest days of his ministry, Spurgeon was convinced that 'A gospel without the Trinity! — it is a rope of sand that cannot hold together... Get the thought of the three persons, and you have the marrow of all divinity. Only know the Father, and know the Son, and know the Holy Ghost to be one, and all things will appear clear.'[50]

In other words, the doctrine of three persons in one Godhead is an essential foundation to both the proclamation of the gospel and the study of theology.

Spurgeon concludes this address with a lengthy reminder of some things that the Spirit will never do. For instance, the Spirit will never bless compromises with doctrinal error or sin — a truth which had been burned afresh into Spurgeon's heart and soul during the Down-Grade controversy. Neither will the Spirit sanction laziness; he is no 'friend of loiterers'.[51] Nor will he have anything to do with those who do not preach Christ. 'If we do not make the Lord Jesus glorious; if we do not lift him high in the esteem of men, if we do not labour to make him King of kings, and Lord of lords; we shall not have the Holy Spirit with us. Vain will be rhetoric, music, architecture, energy, and social status: if our one design be not to magnify the Lord Jesus, we shall work alone and work in vain.'[52]

Conclusion

Many years before, when Spurgeon was in his first pastorate in the hamlet of Waterbeach, he had written a letter to his uncle in which he expressed the wish to be employed not only in Waterbeach but wherever he might be able to serve Christ. 'I often wish', he wrote, 'I were in China, India, or Africa, so that I might preach, preach, preach all day long. It would be sweet to die preaching. But I want more of the Holy Spirit; I do not feel enough — no, not half enough — of his divine energy. "Come, Holy Spirit, come!" Then men must be converted; then the wicked would repent, and the just grow in grace.'[53]

Quite evident in this letter, written when Spurgeon was only nineteen years of age, is Spurgeon's tremendous sensitivity to the absolute necessity of the help of the Holy Spirit in his preaching and ministry. It was a sensitivity that would stay with him throughout his life, as we have seen. It is a sensitivity that explains much about his remarkable ministry. Yet, it is also a sensitivity that serves as an encouragement and a challenge to us in our increasingly godless and needy age. Yes, indeed, 'Where the Spirit of God is, there is power': power to live for Christ and power to bring glory to his person.

Dr Michael A. G. Haykin
Principal of Toronto Baptist Seminary in Toronto, Ontario, Canada, Senior Fellow of the Jonathan Edwards Centre for Reformed Spirituality, Adjunct Professor of Church History at the Southern Baptist Theological Seminary, Louisville, Kentucky, USA.

The Word and the Spirit

Chapter 1

A word with those who wait for signs and wonders

If there should ever be a time when it was not possible for Christians to walk by faith alone, . . . then God would go out of the ordinary way once again, and his people would receive miraculous seals.

1.

A word with those who wait for signs and wonders

This is an evil generation: it seeks a sign — Luke 11:29

A sermon delivered on Lord's Day morning, 31 October 1869, by C. H. Spurgeon, at the Metropolitan Tabernacle, Newington. Sermon No. 898

Reading the Old Testament, we observe that the Lord in times of old condescendingly gave signs to his servants, when he saw that it would be for their good. Moses, when he was called to undertake the great work of bringing the chosen people up out of Egypt and conducting them into the promised land, had a sign given him by which to assure him that he was truly called of God. He put his hand into his bosom, and when he took it out it was leprous, white as snow; he thrust it into his bosom again and again removed it, and, behold, it was whole as the other. He cast his rod upon the earth, and the rod became a serpent, and when he took it by the tail, it stiffened into a rod again. So also in the case of Gideon, when he was commanded to go against the Midianite oppressors of Israel, you remember how his fleece was wet when all around was dry; and how the sign was reversed, and when all around was saturated with moisture, the fleece was dry. In the cases of holy men favoured with signs, there was faith, there was a real desire for more faith, and there was a willing obedience to God. But the work to which the men were called was peculiar, difficult, and even superhuman, and, the flesh being weak, God, in infinite tenderness to the weakness of his servants, gave them signs and wonders by which they might be strengthened. Doubtless if there should again come a necessity for signs to any of God's servants, such tokens would be given to them. If there should ever be a time when it was not possible for Christians to walk by faith alone, or when it would be more to the honour of God that their confidence should be somehow assisted by marvels and tokens, then God would go out of the ordinary way once again, and his people would receive miraculous seals. If it were utterly impossible for the anxious and truly penitent spirit to find rest without a sign, I believe the sign would be given; though I also believe that in no case is such a thing at all necessary under the gospel dispensation, which is so enriched with evidence of the plainest kind that to add more would be to hold a candle to the sun, or pour water into the ocean.

In addition to this first remark, let us add that signs have been given and yet have not wrought faith in those who have seen them; and there is no necessary connection between seeing signs and believing that which the signs attest. Israel in the wilderness saw great marvels wrought by the Lord their God, and yet perished in unbelief. Pharaoh is a still more notable instance — what signs and wonders God wrought in the fields of Zoan! How the Nile was crimsoned into blood, and all Egypt filled with lamentation! The Lord turned the dust of the land into lice, and the ashes therefore into plagues. He brought up frogs into their houses, and locusts devoured their fields. He darkened the heavens at midday, and deluged them with hail and rain such as the land had never seen before. A grievous plague fell upon their cattle, and death upon their first-born; yet all the wonders which God wrought did not soften Pharaoh's heart, and though for a while he trembled, yet again he steeled himself against the God of Israel, and said, 'Who is the Lord, that I should obey his voice?' (Exod. 5:2). If you do not believe Moses and the prophets, if you do not believe in Jesus Christ with the testimonies which are already before you, neither would you believe though one rose from the dead, even though all the plagues of Egypt should be repeated upon you with tenfold fury. There is no necessary connection between the seeing of wonders and believing in God, for we learn clearly from Pharaoh's case, and from many others, that all the displays of wonderful power, either of judgement or of mercy, do not produce faith in unbelieving hearts.

I shall now deal with a class of people very common still among us, exceedingly common in all congregations where the gospel is faithfully preached, whom I shall attempt to describe in the first place, and then go on to deal with them as God shall help me.

1. The people described

First, then, I shall ask your attention while I describe the people who are an evil generation that seek after a sign. We have among us many individuals who are aware that they are sinners, and are conscious of their guiltiness to such an extent as to be very uneasy as to their condition. They clearly perceive that sin will be punished by the Great Judge, and they are much afraid of the wrath to come. They anxiously desire, moreover, to find salvation, and, having long listened to the gospel, they are not ignorant of the way in which salvation is obtained; they understand the gospel, in the letter of it, to the highest degree. They are not unbelievers in any of the doctrines of the gospel; they accept the deity of Christ; they believe him to be truly the Son of God; they believe that he died upon the cross and offered atonement for iniquity. They know, moreover, that this atonement is effectual for the putting away of transgressions, and they are persuaded that if they had an interest in it, it would wash away their sins and would give them peace of mind. You will say to me, 'Knowing all this, of course they are believers in Christ.' No, they are not. We are very hopeful of them; we are at the same time much alarmed about them. They are not believers, for they wilfully persist in demanding some sign or wonder within themselves, or around themselves, before they will personally put their trust in the Lord Jesus. Having been taught all they have been taught, and accepting for truth all that they do accept, the logical inference would be that they trust in Christ and are saved. As illogical as their state is, they still remain unbelievers, with all this belief about them, and justify their remaining in unbelief by telling you that if they felt this, or if they saw that, or if this happened, or if the other thing occurred, then they would believe in Jesus, but not until then.

Expecting remarkable dreams or singular visions

They make different demands. There are some — and these are generally the most uneducated — who expect to experience remarkable dreams or to behold singular visions. I am sometimes astonished that there should still be a notion among our population that a certain kind of dream, especially if it is repeated a number of times, and if it is so vivid as to remain upon the imagination for a long period, is an index of the divine favour. Nothing can be more grossly untrue; nothing can be more baseless and without the shadow of evidence to back it up — and yet many imagine that if they, I was about to say, suffered so grievously from indigestion that their sleep was spoiled by vivid dreams, then they could put their trust in Jesus Christ. The notion is so absurd that we have only to mention it to rational men for them to ridicule it, and yet I have known many who have been, and still are, slaves to this delusion.

Not very long ago, after preaching in a remote country village, I was earnestly sought for as a spiritual adviser by an importunate letter from a woman who ascribed to me much greater wisdom than I ever claimed to possess. I wondered what her spiritual difficulty was, and when I went to her house and found her very sick, I was saddened to find her the victim of a superstition, in which I fear her minister had comforted and so confirmed her. She solemnly informed me that she had seen something standing at night at the bottom of her bed; she was in hopes that it was our blessed Lord, but she could not see his head. As I knew so much of spiritual things, could I tell her who it was? I said I thought she must have hung up her dress on a peg on the wall at the bottom of her bed, and in the dark had mistaken it for an apparition. Of course, that did not satisfy her; I fell at once in her estimation to the dead level of a very carnal-minded man, if not a scoffer, but I could not help it. I could not dally with such ridiculous superstition. I was obliged to tell her it was all nonsense for her to hope for salvation because she was silly enough to fancy that she saw Jesus with her bodily eyes, for the saving sight was a spiritual one. As to the question of the supposed apparition having a head or not, I told her that if she would only use her own head and heart in meditating upon the Word of God, she would be in a far more hopeful condition.

There may have been — I will not deny it, for stranger things have been — there may have been dreams, and even apparitions, which have aroused the conscience and so led to the commencement of spiritual life, in some rare cases where God has chosen specially to interfere, but that these are to be looked for, and to be expected, is a thing as far from truth as the east is from the west. What if you did see anything, or dream anything? What would that prove? Why, it would prove nothing whatever except that you were in an ill state of health, and that your imagination was morbidly active. Put such things away. Such superstitions are fit only for primitive, untaught people who know no better; they are not fit for Christians in this day and age. I mention them, not because I think that any of you have fallen into them, but so that you may deal with them always very rigidly wherever you meet with them. They are superstitions not to be tolerated by Christians, yet there are some who actually will not believe Christ's simple gospel unless some such absurdity as this can be joined to it. May God deliver you from such unbelief.

Feeling a peculiar physical sensation

We have met with others who suppose that in order to be saved they must feel some very peculiar physical sensation. Now, I do not doubt that joy and peace of mind, and the discovery of the gospel when it flashes on the mind for the first time, may produce extraordinary sensations in the body through the force of mental emotion. But I urge you, remember that the grace of our Lord Jesus Christ has nothing to do with nerve and muscle and sinew, and things to be seen and felt in the flesh; the operations of grace are a mental, spiritual work. You must never imagine, when we talk about the heart, that we mean that central organ within us from which the blood circulates; we mean nothing which has to do with this physical body. The work of the Holy Spirit concerns itself with the mind, the affections, the soul, the spirit, and his work is altogether spiritual. God forbid that you should look for any physical work, or strange affection of nerve and sinew, as some have talked of and others have looked for. You must not put physical contortions or sensations as a test before the Lord, and say you will not believe in him otherwise.

Not feeling wretched enough

These I hope are rare cases, but in very frequent instances I have met with people who will not believe in Jesus Christ to the salvation of their souls because they have not felt wretched enough. They have read in certain books of holy men who, when they were seeking a Saviour, were broken in pieces under the ponderous hammer of the law. They turn to such biographies, and they find the subjects of them uttering language similar to the book of Job, or to the words of Jeremiah in Lamentations. Now these were good and holy men, and the way by which they were led to Christ was a way trodden by many feet, but these persons say, 'Unless I can feel just this, unless I can be led into despair, unless I can be tempted to destroy myself, unless I become so despondent that I am fitter for a lunatic asylum than to be in my own family, I cannot believe in Jesus Christ.' Ah! Poor demented one, to desire misery, and to make your own wretchedness, and even your own unbelieving and wicked thoughts of God, to be a kind of preparation, for faith in Jesus Christ! It is a most insanely wicked thing, and yet many, many, many persist in unbelief because they think they are not yet wretched enough.

Not feeling happy enough

Running to the other extreme, I have met with others who would not simply trust Christ because they were not happy enough. They have heard of the Christian's joys, and the peace like a river that evermore abides, and they have said, 'If I could get this peace, if this deep calm ruled in my spirit, then I could believe' — as much as to say, 'If I saw the wheat full grown in the fields of my soul, then I would begin to sow', whereas the sowing must precede the reaping. 'If I had within me the flower in all its beauty and bloom, then I would begin to plant the root', whereas the root must always precede the flower. Peace of mind is the result of faith, but they demand that they should have the result of faith before they exercise faith; in short, they come to God and ask for the wages before the work is begun, demanding peace before they will believe. Believe me, if any of you thus act wilfully and strangely, you must not suppose that

God will turn aside from his wise proceedings to gratify your whims. No, you may tempt the Lord, but he is not tempted by any man. What folly it is — and yet, folly as it is, how common it is on all sides!

Not able to pray eloquently

I have met with some who would not believe in Christ because they could not pray eloquently. 'Oh,' they have said, 'if I could pray like so-and-so, to whom we have listened with the greatest pleasure at the prayer meeting, then I could put my trust in Christ, and there would be some hope for me!' Now, praying fluently is sometimes only the result of oratorical gifts, and if you will never believe in Christ till you get oratorical gifts, then how foolish you are to shut yourself out from heaven because you cannot play the orator; and because you cannot be a preacher, refuse to be a saint! True, fluency in prayer may also be the result of great depth of piety, but you expect to have great depth of piety before you even have the beginning of grace in your soul. Before you will put your trust in Christ and become a baby in his family, you claim to be a man six feet high. Before you will learn the 'ABC' of the language of Canaan, you declare that you must be able to sound its very hardest syllables and pronounce its most difficult sentences. That which is frequently the result of years of training and long habit of deep, solitary contemplation, you expect to leap into at once, or else you refuse to be saved! Oh, madness, to what height will you not mount!

Requiring instant perfection

I have known others who must feel precisely like certain eminent saints have felt many years after their conversion, or else they cannot believe that they are saved. They will reach down the life of some holy man who had mastered his passions by long years of mortification, who had come to live near to God, and whose life was the heavenly life on earth, and they will mentally vow, 'I must be just like this man or else', they say, 'I cannot believe in Jesus.' They say, in fact, to the heavenly Physician, 'I am sick and ready to die, but, Good Physician, you must make me as strong as Samson at once and on the spot, or else I will not receive your medicine,' just as if the perfect spiritual cure of the soul were not a lifelong work of grace. They expect to be made perfect in an instant, or they will not trust the ever-faithful Saviour. They look for the mature fruits of autumn in the early spring, and before they bear even so much as a bud or blossom, they must have the full ripe fruit, or else they will not believe. Well, this is marvellous, and truly, if there is anything amazing on earth beside the mercy of God, it is the perversity of man, and the strange way in which unbelief will dare impudently to set up one demand after another as an excuse for rejecting the Lord Jesus Christ.

Desiring some mysterious phenomenon

We have met this mischief at other times in a somewhat indescribable shape. 'Sir,' says the young convert, 'you tell me that if I simply put my trust in Jesus I shall be saved, but is not salvation a great mystery?' Our reply must honestly be, 'No doubt it is.' Well, then, they determine to wait until they are the subjects of some singular feeling, some mysterious phenomenon within themselves. It is not to be denied that the work of grace by the Holy Spirit in the soul is the highest of all mysteries, but it is also never to be forgotten that it is one of the grandest of all simplicities. The mysteries of the church of Rome are mock mysteries rendered dark by the veil which she casts over truth. By her incantations, her paraphernalia, her performances and her use of a strange tongue, that which is simple is darkened into a mimic mystery, for what is really in it is a plain lie for thoughtful men to laugh at. This is a kind of mystery of which the gospel knows nothing. The mysteries of regeneration are not artificial but natural.

Now all natural mysteries in the world are, from another point of view, clear simplicities. Light — we know what it is, we see it every day; it is the greatest of all mysteries, yet practically it is the commonest of all simplicities. When the sun scatters the darkness, there is no mystery about it. Or when we light a candle, there is no need of wonder. Light is a wondrous mystery, yet to obtain it the least educated need not go to school. The electric telegraph is practically, as a matter of everyday use, so simplified that a lad may officiate at the instrument, and yet it remains, and ever will remain, a mystery.

Understand that such is the mystery of regeneration. It is so mysterious that no one can explain it, but it is so simple that anyone who believes in Christ has experienced it already. It is so mysterious that if the most learned tomes were composed to define it, all the writers in the world might fail in the definition, but it also is so simple that anyone who believes in Jesus Christ is born of God. There is nothing mysterious about it, I was about to say, in the artificial meaning of that word 'mystery'. The only mystery lies in the operation of the Holy Spirit, whose coming and going we cannot comprehend. If you believe, you have felt the mystery. If you trust Jesus, you possess mystery. All that is meant in regeneration, all that is wrapped up in the work of the Holy Spirit, actually belongs to every soul that has believed in Jesus Christ and in him only. But I know what it is: you will go to Abanah and Pharpar, rivers of Damascus, but you will not come to the blood of Christ and wash and be clean; you will say, 'Indeed, I said to myself, "He will surely come out to me, and stand and call on the name of the Lord his God, and wave his hand over the place, and heal the leprosy"' (2 Kings 5:11), but you cannot accept the simple word, 'Believe and live,' so grand in its simplicity. Most men reject the gospel for that very reason of its simplicity. Signs and wonders they will still demand; something artificially mysterious their soul still craves after; but the naked grandeur of the sublime mystery of faith they cannot perceive. Their folly is clear enough to all men that have eyes. I have just described the character, and if any have felt themselves portrayed in these words, I hope they will prepare their hearts for what will follow, and be willing to receive my Master's word.

2. The folly of their conduct

I shall now, secondly, show the folly of such conduct. My dear friend, I anxiously desire that you may be saved this very day. You are seeking a sign, one of these which I have described, or some other.

Unnecessary signs

You seek what is quite unnecessary. What do you want a sign for? You want, you say, a token of God's love. What token of God's love to you can ever be wanted, now that he has given his only begotten Son, first to live on earth, and then to die in extreme pain, the just for the unjust, 'that whoever believes in him should not perish but have everlasting life'? (John 3:16). I blush for you, that you should ask any token of God's love while Jesus Christ is before you, for here is such love as nothing else can ever equal. What do you want a sign for? Why, to show, you say, that there is mercy for you. How do you need that? The very fact that you are alive shows how merciful God is! Had he been unmerciful, he would have cut you down long ago, for what are you but a cumberer of the ground, with your heart full of evil devices at this very moment, at enmity against him? I know you are in that condition, or otherwise you would not be so hard to lead to faith, yet you are spared by his mercy. Is that not proof enough? And, moreover, the gospel is preached to you. You are told that 'He who believes and is baptized will be saved' (Mark 16:16). He must be a good God who lets you hear such a gospel, and who bids me plead with you, as though Christ pleaded with you, that you would lay hold of him.

Why, the gospel itself is the greatest of signs and wonders. What do you want more that that? 'Oh,' you say, 'can the gospel save me?' My dear friend, you do not want any sign to prove that. You have your own relatives, your own sons and daughters who have been saved. You are a witness to what grace has done for them; what more evidence can you require? Remember the dying bed of your godly mother; recollect the joyous departure of your brother, or your converted child. Evidently grace did wonders for them. What more do you want to convince you? Mind you, if you did not believe that Jesus is the Son of God, if you did not believe that his blood could cleanse from sin, I might talk somewhat differently to you; but you do believe all this, and I say, in the name of all that is reasonable, what makes you ask for any greater sign than the signs which God has already given you? You are seeking for altogether unnecessary things.

Useless signs

You are also asking for useless signs. What evidence could there be now, for instance, in mere dejection of spirit? You want to feel miserable, you say. What evidence would that be of your salvation? It seems to me that you are like a man who was to say that he would catch hold of a rope if he could sink so many fathoms deeper in the ocean, or that he would avail himself of a dispensary if his disease were so much worse. How strange that a rational man should talk this way! Despair is no help to faith. Sinful doubts cannot assist you to come to Christ; they may most effectually keep you from him.

> Why those fears, poor trembling sinner;
> Why those anxious, gloomy fears?
> Doubts and fears can never save thee,

Life is never won by tears;
'Tis believing,
Which the soul to Christ endears

Tears, though flowing like a river,
Never can one sin efface;
Jesus' tears would not avail thee —
Blood alone can meet thy case;
Fly to Jesus!
Life is found in his embrace.

Or you may say, 'I have desired to feel ecstatic joy.' But if you did, how could that help you to believe in Christ? Your joy might be no more than what worldlings feel when their wealth increases; it might spring of mere excitement; it might all be based upon a lie, and your joy might be your damnation. Oh man, Christ is worthy of confidence, but your joys and your sorrows are not worthy of confidence. They may be good, or they may be bad; they may be hopeful, or they may be delusive. Why then do you look at them, or seek another foundation than that which God has laid? Your feelings are fickle things. Believe and live.

Unreasonable signs

Are you not also seeking most unreasonable things? To ask a sign from God when he pledges his word seems to me to be out of all reason. You are a beggar, remember, and we have an old proverb that beggars must not be choosers. Above all, how dare a beggar demand a sign before he will receive alms? I am walking in the street, and am accosted by a hungry man. If I offer him a loaf of bread, is he to refuse to take it unless I will fly in the air or help him to turn a stone into bread? 'Let the man starve, sir,' you will say, 'if he is so unreasonable as to demand a sign.' And yet that is just like you. You will not take the mercy which the gospel freely offers you, which God even commands you to accept — you will not take it unless some astonishing sign or wonder is wrought in you.

Signs not promised

Let your folly appear still further when I remind you that you are asking for signs which God has not promised. God has promised that everyone that believes in Jesus Christ shall live. He has promised to hear prayer, but he has never promised to give any one of you a sign or a wonder. Yet you will ask him to give you a sign which he has never promised, and dare not ask him to give you eternal life, which he has promised. Folly indeed!

Harmful signs

Some of you are seeking for injurious signs. That depression of spirit which some think would be such an encouragement to them — why, it is even sinful. How should I ask a sinful thing of God? To be distracted in my mind, to be so depressed and melancholy as to make myself and all my household miserable — is that a good thing? It is a great sin against God. Am I then to ask God to give me this sign in order to help me to believe? Thoughts of suicide — why, my brothers, they are awful, they are not to be allowed! There is murder in them. He that even thinks of them has committed murder already in his heart.

And are these terrible, devilish things to help you to believe? Why, they would just drive you into hell. How can they help you to heaven? You are asking for that which would be your ruin. You ask for a scorpion, you ask for a stone, you ask for a serpent — and then you think that after having all these evil things you would be more fit to receive the bread of the divine blessing. God will deny you, I trust, what you so foolishly ask for.

Oh, be content to be led in a gentler way; be willing to be blown to Christ by the soft south wind — do not ask for tempests. Be satisfied to be drawn by the cords of love and by the bands of a man — do not demand whips and chains. Do not enquire for the thunders and lightnings of Sinai; be satisfied with the dovelike notes of Calvary.

Hark! The voice of Jesus calling,
'Come, thou laden, come to me;
I have rest and peace to offer,
Rest, poor labouring one, for thee;
Take salvation,
Take it now, and happy be.'

Life is found alone in Jesus,
Only there 'tis offered thee —
Offer'd without price or money,
'Tis the gift of God sent free;
Take salvation,
Take it now, and happy be.

Unprecedented signs

Remember that some of you who are not believing are seeking signs which others have never had. To give you an instance or two: there stood the prodigal son feeding the swine, so hungry that he would gladly have filled his belly with the husks. The thought crossed his mind, 'I will arise and go to my father' (Luke 15:18). What sign did he have? He sets off to seek his father's face. What sign did he have, I say? There does not appear to have been even an invitation sent, but he sought his father and he found forgiveness.

Take another case. Christ has likened seeking souls to the widow who sought help from the unjust judge (Luke 18). She cried to him; she continued to cry to him, until she gained her suit. But what sign did she receive? If she had any sign, it was all negative, all from the opposite quarter; yet on she went.

Look at the Canaanite woman (Matt. 15). She desired that her daughter might be healed. What sign did she have? Christ said, 'It is not good to take the children's bread and throw it to the little dogs' (v. 26). Instead of a sign to help her, it was a hard word to discourage her, but yet she won her suit. And why not you, my readers? Why not you? The poor woman who touched the hem of Christ's garment in the press — what sign did she have of his willingness to help her? It was her own earnest, intense desire, and her faith in Jesus that made her touch the hem out of which the virtue came. Do not wait then for signs to be given to you when they have not been given to others, but do as others have done, and obtain a blessing like theirs.

3. The sin of seeking after a sign

I now want to take a little more of your time, while I lay bare your sins, your grievous sins, and I urge you to pay very serious attention to my words.

Making God a liar

In the first place, you make God a liar. Is this not the testimony of the Holy Spirit: 'He who does not believe God has made him a liar'? (1 John 5:10). How do we treat liars? If they tell us a thing, we say, 'I am doubtful of it'; we want more evidence. Now, I feel persuaded that many of you may respect even me so well that if I made a statement you would accept it without any further evidence; but here is the everlasting God, who declares that whoever trusts his Son shall be saved, and you practically give him the lie. If you believed what he testifies, since you want to be saved, you would surely trust his Son. Yet you practically say, 'We do not believe it; we do not believe it; we want more evidence; we want a sign and a wonder.' You make God a liar.

Insulting God's sovereignty

In the next place, you insult God's sovereignty. He has a right to give signs, or not, as he wills, but you say, as it were, 'You shall give me a sign, or else I will be damned. I will not have your mercy if I cannot have it in my own way. Great God, I will not be saved unless I can feel as I want to feel. I have a whim in my mind as to how the work of grace is to be wrought, and if it does not begin as I think best, I would sooner make my bed in hell than accept your Son.' Is the preacher being too hard with you? Ah, it is love that makes me hard! In truth, it is you who are hard with God and hard with your own souls. Oh, fling away this accursed pride of yours, and kiss his silver sceptre, and say, 'Lord, save me as you will. I believe. Help my unbelief.'

Acting like an idolater

I must tell you what is more: you are acting the part of an idolater. What does an idolater do? He says, 'I cannot believe in an unseen God; I must have a golden calf or an image that I can see with my eyes and touch with my hand.' You say just the same. You cannot believe God's naked word; you demand something you can feel, something you can see. That is sheer idolatry. Do you not see it? You make your own feelings and emotions, or strange impressions, to be more worthy of trust than even God himself; you make them idols, and put them in God's place. You, so far as you can, undeify the Deity. Oh, tremble at such a crime as this!

Crucifying the Saviour

Do you not see, moreover, that you crucify the Saviour? Those who nailed his hands to the tree were not greater sinners, even if they were as great, than you are who say to him, 'Bleeding Saviour, I believe that you have died on the cross; I believe that your blood could cleanse sin, but I cannot trust you to do it. I have no confidence in you; I cannot, will not trust you. I trust my husband, but I cannot trust my Saviour; I trust my child, but I cannot trust my God; I trust my minister, but I cannot trust the Son of God exalted in the highest heavens.' Why, this is crucifying him — this is treating him as only a dog should be treated. I do not know what can be worse than this. Nails in his hands are not more cruel than this mistrust of his deep love and his divine power. 'Ah,' says one, 'I do not mean that; but I want to see the work of the Holy Spirit in my soul.' Ah, then, I have another charge to bring against you — you are wanting to trust in the work of the Holy Spirit, instead of trusting in the work of Jesus Christ.

Now, there is no text in all the Bible that tells you to make the work of the Holy Spirit the foundation of our confidence. Nowhere is it set forth as the ground for a sinner's reliance; it occupies quite another place. If you try to put the work of the Spirit where the work of Christ should be, you grieve the Holy Spirit, for the very last thing that the Holy Spirit ever would do would be to supplant the Lamb of God. It is his office and mission to glorify Christ; how, then, shall he supplant him? When you say, 'I cannot trust the blood, I cannot trust the righteousness of Christ; I must have something from the Holy Spirit to trust to,' you do, as it were, try to make a clash between the work of the Holy Spirit and the work of Christ, and this grieves the Spirit to the last degree.

4. The danger of seeking after a sign

I have thought over this subject carefully, and I have tried to deal with it earnestly, but I am conscious when I have done my best that you will go on in this folly and still continue in this sin. Yet I do pray the Holy Spirit that it may not be so, for now in the closing paragraphs I desire to show you your danger as I have shown you your folly and sin.

The danger of death

My dear friends, you are in danger of death. You admit that, and now suppose you die in the state you are in. Why, you are almost saved; you are awakened, you are aroused, you have many good desires; but a man who is only almost saved will be altogether damned. There was a householder who almost bolted his door at night, but the thief came in; a prisoner was condemned to be hanged, and was almost pardoned, but he hung on the gallows; a ship was almost saved from shipwreck, but she went to the bottom with all hands on board; a fire was almost extinguished, but it consumed a city; a man who has almost decided remains to perish in the flames of hell.

So is it with you: unless you believe, all these things which you possess of good desire and emotion will be of no service to you at all, for 'He that believes not shall be damned' (Mark 16:16, AV). Remember, friend, you may be damned before the sun goes down today; the flames of hell may enclose you before the sun rises on another day. Oh, seek the Saviour now while the gospel message comes with fresh power today. 'Believe on the Lord Jesus Christ, and you will be saved' (Acts 16:31), for 'He who believes and is baptized will be saved' (Mark 16:16).

> Soon that voice will cease its calling,
> Now it speaks, and speaks to thee;
> Sinner, heed the gracious message,

To the blood for refuge flee;
Take salvation,
Take it now, and happy be.

The danger of a seared conscience

There is one other thing of which you are in danger, namely, that if you are spared for years to come, through long procrastination your conscience may nevertheless become seared as with a hot iron. If you do believe today, whatever you may have been, your sins are all forgiven in a moment; if you do now look to Christ upon Calvary and trust your soul with him, you will now live, for:

There is life in a look at the Crucified One,
There is life at this moment for thee.

But if you look to your good works, to your preparations, to your fears, to your joys — if, indeed, you do look to anything but Christ, it may be that the Holy Spirit will never strive with you again, that your conscience will become hardened and that you, being given up to your idols, will perish, utterly perish, under the sound of the gospel; perish with the light of the gospel shining on your eyeballs; perish of the serpent-bite while the brazen serpent is lifted high; perish of thirst when the water of life runs rippling at your feet, because you are not content to stoop down and take it as God presents it to you. Oh, that you would this very day end these follies and these sins, believing in Jesus Christ, through the power of the Holy Spirit!

Jesus, the eternal Son of God,
Whom seraphim obey,
The bosom of the Father leaves,
And enters human clay.

The Word and the Spirit

Chapter 2

True unity promoted

The destruction of every sort of union which is not based on truth is a preliminary to the edification of the unity of the Spirit.

2.
True unity promoted

Endeavouring to keep the unity of the Spirit in the bond of peace — Eph. 4:3

A sermon delivered on Lord's Day morning, 1 January 1865, by C. H. Spurgeon, at the Metropolitan Tabernacle, Newington. Sermon No. 607

For several years I have received my morning's text for the first Lord's Day in the year from an esteemed brother, a clergyman of the Church of England. This year he very kindly sends me this verse, which I hope will be useful to us all, reminding us of our former faults and of our present duty in the matter of 'endeavouring to keep the unity of the Spirit in the bond of peace'.

The Pope has lately been most lustily cursing us all. According to his nature, of course, must be his utterances. We could not expect a blessing where no blessing abides, and, if we get a curse, we only receive a polluted stream from a polluted fountain. It is an old saying that 'England never prospers so well as when the Pope curses her.' I hope to see a year of great prosperity this year. Let the poor deluded priest curse as long as he will; our God shall turn it into a blessing. In former days, when some of the churches of Christ began to shake off the yoke of popedom from their necks, the plea urged against reformation was the necessity of maintaining unity: 'You must bear with this ceremony and that dogma; no matter how antichristian and unholy, you must bear with it, "endeavouring to keep the unity of the Spirit in the bond of peace".' So spoke the old serpent in those early days: 'The church is one; woe unto those who shall create schism!' It may be true that Mary is set up in the place of Christ, that images are worshipped, cast-off clouts and rotten rags adored and pardons bought and sold for crimes of every kind; it may be that the so-called church has become an abomination and a nuisance upon the face of the earth; but still, 'endeavouring to keep the unity of the Spirit in the bond of peace', you must lie down, restrain the testimony of the Spirit of God within you, keep his truth under a bushel, and let the lie prevail. This was the grand sophistry of the Church of Rome. When, however, she could not seduce men by talking of love and union, she took upon herself to use her natural tone of voice, and cursed heartily right and left; and let her curse till she expires!

Brothers, there was no force in the argument of the papist, if you will look at the text for a moment. The text bids us endeavour to keep the unity of the Spirit, but it does not tell us to endeavour to maintain the unity of evil, the unity of superstition, or the unity of spiritual tyranny. The unity of error, of false doctrine, of priestcraft, may have in it the spirit of Satan; we do not doubt that; but we do utterly deny that it is the unity of the Spirit of God. The unity of evil we are to break down by every weapon which our hand can grasp. The unity of the Spirit which we are to maintain and foster is quite another thing. Remember that we are forbidden to do evil that good may come. But it is to do evil: to restrain the witness of the Spirit of God within us; to conceal any truth which we have learned by revelation of God; to hold back from testifying for God's truth and Word against the sin and folly of man's inventions, would be sin of the blackest hue. We dare not commit the sin of quenching the Holy Spirit, even though it were with the view of promoting unity. But the unity of the Spirit never requires any sinful support; that is maintained not by suppressing truth but by publishing it abroad. The unity of the Spirit has for its pillars, among other things, the witnessing of spiritually enlightened saints to the one faith which God has revealed in his Word. That is quite another unity which would gag our mouths and turn us all into dumb, driven cattle, to be fed or slaughtered at the will of priestly masters. Dr McNeil[1] has said, very properly, that a man can scarcely be an earnest Christian in the present day without being a controversialist. We are sent forth today as sheep in the midst of wolves: can there be agreement? We are kindled as lamps in the midst of darkness: can there be concord?

Has not Christ himself said, 'Do not think that I came to bring peace on earth. I did not come to bring peace but a sword' (Matt. 10:34)? You understand how all this is the truest method of endeavouring to keep the unity of the Spirit; for Christ the man of war is Jesus the peacemaker; but in order to the creation of lasting, spiritual peace, the phalanx of evil must be broken and the unity of darkness dashed to shivers. I pray God forever to preserve us from a unity in which truth is considered valueless, in which principle gives place to policy, in which the noble and masculine virtues which adorn the Christian hero are to be supplemented by an effeminate affectation of charity. May the Lord deliver us from indifference to his Word and will, for this creates the cold unity of masses of ice frozen into an iceberg, chilling the air for miles around: the unity of the dead as they sleep in their graves, contending for nothing, because they have neither part nor lot in all that belongs to living men.

There is a unity which is seldom broken, the unity of devils, who, under the service of their great liege master, never disagree and quarrel: from this terrible unity keep us, oh God of heaven! The unity of locusts who have one common object, the glutting of themselves to the ruin of all around; the unity of the waves of Tophet's fire, sweeping myriads into deeper misery: from this also, oh King of heaven, save us for ever! May God perpetually send some prophet who shall cry aloud to the world, 'Your covenant with death will be annulled, and your agreement with Sheol will not stand' (Isa. 28:18).

May there ever be found some men, though they may be as rough as Amos or as stern as Haggai, who shall denounce again and again all league with error and all compromise with sin, and declare that these are the abhorrence of God. Never dream that holy contention is at all a violation of my text. The destruction of every sort of union which is not based on truth is a preliminary to the edification of the unity of the Spirit. We must first sweep away these walls of untempered mortar — these tottering fences of man's building — before there can be room to lay the goodly stones of Jerusalem's walls one upon the other for lasting and enduring prosperity. In this spirit I have spoken to clear a way to reach my text.

It is clear from the text that there is a unity of the Spirit to be kept; secondly, that it needs keeping; and, thirdly, that a bond is to be used. When we have enlarged upon these points, we shall use the text in its practical application, first to Christians in their connection with other churches, and then to members of the same church in their connection with each other.

1. A unity of the Spirit worthy to be kept

First, there is a unity of the Spirit of which the text speaks, which is worthy to be kept. You will observe that it is not an ecclesiastical unity; it is not endeavouring to keep the unity of the denomination, the community, the diocese, the parish — no, it is 'endeavouring to keep the unity of the Spirit'. Men speak of the Episcopal Church, the Wesleyan Church, or the Presbyterian Church. Now I do not hesitate to say that there is nothing whatever in Scripture at all parallel to such language; for there I read of the seven churches in Asia, the church in Corinth,

Philippi, Antioch, etc. In England, if I speak according to the Word of God, there are some thousands of churches holding the Episcopal form of government; in Scotland, some thousands of godly churches ordered according to Presbyterian rule; among the Wesleyans, churches adhering to the form of government first carried out by Mr Wesley. But it is not according to the method of Scripture but only according to human invention to speak of a whole cluster of churches as one *church*. Although much inclined myself to a Presbyterian union among our churches, I perceive in holy Scripture that each church is separate and distinct from every other church; the whole being connected by those diverse bonds and ligaments which keep all the separate members together, but not so connected as to run into one another to lose their separateness and individuality. There is nothing in Scripture which says, 'endeavouring to keep up your ecclesiastical arrangements for centralization'; but the exhortation runs thus: 'endeavouring to keep the unity of the Spirit'.

Not the uniformity of the Spirit

Again, you will observe it does not say, 'endeavouring to keep the uniformity of the Spirit'. The Spirit does not recognize uniformity. The analogy of his work in nature is against it. The flowers are not all tinted with the same hue, nor do they exhale the same odours. There is variety everywhere in the work of God. If I glance at providence I do not perceive that any two events happen after the same form — the page of history is varied. If therefore I look into the church of God, I do not expect to find that all Christians pronounce the same 'Shibboleth' (Judg. 12:6) or see with the same eyes. The same 'one Lord, one faith, one baptism, one God and Father of all', we rejoice to recognize, but I find nothing in Scripture as to uniformity of dress, liturgical verbiage, or form of worship. Men may pray acceptably standing, sitting, kneeling, or lying with their faces upon the earth; they may meet with Jesus by the river's side, in the temple porch, in a prison, or in a private house; and they may be one in the same Spirit although the one regards a day, and the other does not regard it.

Unity of the Spirit described

But what is this unity of the Spirit? I trust, dear brothers, that we know it by having it in possession, for it is most certain that we cannot *keep* the unity of the Spirit if we do not already have it. Let us ask ourselves the question, 'Do we have the unity of the Spirit?' None can have it but those who have the Spirit, and the Spirit dwells only in new-born believing souls. By virtue of his having the Spirit, the believer is in union with every other spiritual man, and this is the unity which he is to endeavour to keep. This unity of the Spirit is manifested in love. A husband and wife may be, through providence, cast hundreds of miles from one another, but there is a unity of spirit in them because their hearts are one. We, brothers, are divided by many thousands of miles from the saints in Australia, America and the South Sea, but, loving as brothers, we feel the unity of the Spirit. I was never a member of a church meeting in the backwoods of America; I never worshipped God with the Samoans, or with my brothers in New Zealand; but notwithstanding all this, I feel the unity of the Spirit in my soul with them, and everything which concerns their spiritual welfare is interesting to me.

This unity of the Spirit is caused by a similarity of nature. Find a drop of water glittering in the rainbow, leaping in the cataract, rippling in the rivulet, lying silent in the stagnant pool, or dashing in spray against the vessel's side: that water claims kinship with every drop of water the wide world over because it is the same in its elements. In the same way there is a unity of the Spirit which we cannot imitate, which consists in our being 'begotten … again to a living hope through the resurrection of Jesus Christ from the dead' (1 Peter 1:3), bearing in us the Holy Spirit as our daily quickener, and walking in the path of faith in the living God. Here is the unity of spirit, a unity of life, nature working itself out in love. This is sustained daily by the Spirit of God. He who makes us one, keeps us one.

Every member of my body must have a communion with every other member of my body. I say *must*. The question never arises that I know of between the members of my body whether they will do so or not; as long as there is life in my frame every separate portion of my body must have communion with every other portion of it. Here is my finger — I may discolour it with some noxious drug; my head may not approve of the staining of my finger; my head may suggest a thousand ways by which that finger ought to be put through a purgation, and this may be all right and proper; but my head never says, 'I will cut off that finger from communion.' My tongue speaks loudly against the noxious fluid which has done my finger mischief and has blistered it so as to cause pain to the whole body, yet the head cannot say, 'I will have that finger cut off', unless the body is willing to be for ever mutilated and incomplete.

Now, it is not possible to mutilate the body of Christ. Christ does not lose his members or cast off parts of his mystical body. Therefore it never ought to enter the head of any Christian whether or not he shall have communion in spirit with any other Christian, for he cannot do without it; as long as he lives he must have it. This does not stop him from boldly denouncing the error into which his brother may have fallen, or in avoiding his intimate acquaintance while he continues to sin; but it does forbid the thought that we can ever really sever any true believer from Christ, or even from us, if we are in Christ Jesus.

The unity of the Spirit is preserved, then, by the Holy Spirit infusing daily life-floods into the one mystical body. As the life-floods become stronger, that union becomes proportionally more manifest. Let a spirit of prayer be poured out on all our churches; conventionalities will be dashed down, divisions will be forgotten, and, locked in each other's arms, the people of God will show to the world that they are one in Christ Jesus.

There are some points in which this unity of the Spirit is certain to discover itself. In prayer, how truly Montgomery[2] puts it:

> The saints in prayer appear as one;
> In word, and deed, and mind,
> While with the Father and the Son,
> Sweet fellowship they find.

There is a unity of praise too. Our hymn books differ very little after all; we still sing the same song, the praise of the same Saviour.

This unity will soon discover itself in co-working: they have a union in their conflict with the common foe, and in their contention for the common truth. This will lead to communion — I do not mean sitting down to the same table to eat bread and drink wine; that is only the outward union — but I mean that communion which consists in heart beating true to heart, and in the feeling that they are one in Christ Jesus. It was a motto with Bucer[3] 'to love all in whom we could see anything of Christ Jesus'. Make this your motto, brother in Christ; do not make your love an excuse for not offering stern rebuke, but rebuke because you love.

Some people think that unless you smooth your tongue and cover your words with sugar, no matter though it may be sugar of lead — unless you cringe, and compliment, and conceal, there is no love in your heart; but I trust it will be our privilege to show in our own persons, some of us, how sternly we can dissent and yet love; how truly be Nonconformists to our brethren's error, and yet in our very nonconformity prove our affection to them and to our common Master.

It is said of some men that they appear to have been born upon the mountains of Bether, for they do nothing but cause division; and that they have been baptized in the waters of Meribah, for they delight in causing strife. This is not the case with the genuine Christian; he cares only for the truth, for his Master, for the love of souls, and when these things are not imperilled, his own private likes or dislikes never affect him. He loves to see another church prosper as much as his own: so long as he can know that Christ is glorified, it is a matter of comparative indifference to him by what minister God's arm is made bare, in what place souls are converted, or to what particular form of worship men may be committed.

Yet he ever holds to this, that there is no unity of the Spirit where there is a lie in the case; that where the souls of men are concerned he would be a traitor to God if he did not bear witness against the error which damns and testify to the truth which saves; and where the crown jewels of his Master's kingdom are concerned he does not dare traitorously hold his tongue. Though his fellow subjects cast his name out as evil, he counts it all joy so long as he is faithful to his Master and discharges his conscience as before the Judge of the living and the dead.

2. The difficulty of keeping the unity of the Spirit

Secondly, this unity needs keeping. It is a very difficult thing to maintain, for several reasons. Our sins would, very naturally, break it. If we were all angels, we would keep the unity of the Spirit, and not need even the exhortation to do so. Alas! We are proud, and pride is the mother of division. 'Diotrephes, who loves to have the pre-eminence' (3 John 1:9) is very sure to head a faction. Envy, too — how that separated true friends! When I cannot be satisfied with anything which is not hammered on my anvil or run in my mould; when another man's candle grieves me because it gives more light than mine; and when another man troubles me because he has more grace than I have — Oh! There is no unity in this case. Anger — what a deadly foe that is to unity, when we cannot brook the smallest disrespect; when the slightest thing brings the blood into our face; when we speak unadvisedly with our lips. Surely I do not need to read the long list of sins which spoil this unity of the Spirit, for they are many. Oh, may God cast them out from us, for only then can we keep the unity of the Spirit. But, beloved, even our virtues may make it difficult for us to keep this unity.

Luther[4] is brave and bold, hot and impetuous; he is just the man to lead the van and clear the way for the Reformation. Calvin[5] is logical, clear, cool, precise; he seldom speaks rashly. It is not in the order of things that Luther and Calvin should always agree. Their very virtues cause them to fall out, and, consequently, Luther, in a bad temper, calls Calvin a pig and a devil; and, although Calvin once replied, 'Luther may call me what he will, but I will always call him a dear servant of Christ', John Calvin knew how to pierce Luther under the fifth rib when he was in the humour.

In those days the courtesies of Christians to one another were generally of the iron-gauntlet order, rather than the naked hand, for all were so much called to war for the sake of the truth that even their fellow soldiers were treated with suspicion. It may be with us that the very watchfulness of truth, which is so valuable, may make us suspect where there is no need for suspicion, and our courage may take us as sometimes a fiery horse has carried a young warrior beyond where he intended to have ridden, where he may be taken prisoner to his own damage. We must watch, the best of us must watch, lest we fight the Lord's battles with Satan's weapons, and so even from love to God and his truth, violate the unity of the Spirit.

The unity of the Spirit ought to be kept, dear friends, because Satan is so busy to mar it. He knows that the greatest glory of Christ will spring from the unity of his church. 'That they all may be one, as you, Father, are in me, and I in you; that they also may be one in us, that the world may believe that you sent me'

(John 17:21). There is no church happiness where there is not church unity. Let a church be disaffected and divided, and the schism in the body is death to all hallowed fellowship. We cannot enjoy communion with each other unless our hearts are one. How feebly our work for God is done when we are not agreed! The enemy cannot desire a better ally than strife in the midst of our camp. 'Can you not agree', said a warrior of old, 'when your enemy is in sight?' Christians, can you not agree to keep the unity of the Spirit when a destroying Satan is ever on the watch, seeking to drag immortal souls down to perdition? We must be more diligent in this matter; we must seek to purge out from ourselves everything which would divide, and to have in our hearts every holy thought which would tend to unite us with our brothers. I am not to say, when I join a Christian church, 'I am quite certain I shall never break its unity.' I am to suspect myself of a tendency to that evil, and I am to watch with all diligence that I keep the unity of the Spirit.

3. The bond of peace provided

In the third place, in order to the keeping of this, there is a bond provided, the bond of peace. Beloved, there should be much peace, perfect peace, unbounded peace between the people of God. We are not foreigners; we are 'fellow citizens with the saints and members of the household of God' (Eph. 2:19). Realize your fellow-citizenship; do not treat Christian people as foreigners, and this bond of fellow-citizenship will be one bond of peace. You are not enemies; men may be fellow citizens and yet hate one another. You are friends, you are all friends to Christ, and in him you are all friends to one another; let that be another bond. But you go farther; you are not mere friends, you are brothers, born of the same parent, filled with the same life; and should not this be a bond? See that you do not fall out by the way; do not strive one with another, for you are brothers.

This is not all; you are nearer than this; you are members of the same body. Should this mysterious union fail to be a bond of peace to you? Will you, being the foot, contend with the eye? Or will you, being the eye, contend with the hand, and say, 'I have no need of you'? (1 Cor. 12:21). If it is indeed the truth, and not a fiction, that we are members of his body, of his flesh, and of his bones, and since the joints and bones in other men's bodies do not disagree, let it never be said of the mystical body of our blessed Lord, that there was such a monstrous thing in it that the various parts would not work together, but fell to battling one with another.

I believe I have brought out the meaning of the text. There is a unity of the Spirit which is worthy to be kept — we ought to keep it — we must try to keep it in the bond of peace.

4. The practical conclusion of keeping the unity of the Spirit

Now we come to the practical conclusion of the subject: first, in the connection of one church with another, and, secondly, in the connection of one church member with another.

The connection of one church with another

It is not a desirable thing that all churches should melt into one another and become one. The complete fusion of all churches into one ecclesiastical corporation would inevitably produce another form of popery, since history teaches us that large ecclesiastical bodies grow more or less corrupt as a matter of course. Huge spiritual corporations are, as a whole, the strongholds of tyranny and the refuges of abuse, and it is only a matter of time when they shall break into pieces. Disruption and secession must occur, and will occur, where a unity is attempted which is not meant in God's Word. But it will be a blessed thing when all the churches walk together in the unity of the Spirit:

- when a church which been baptized into the Lord Jesus Christ, although it laments the neglect of that ordinance by others, nevertheless feels that the unity of the Spirit is not to be broken, and holds out its right hand to all who love our Lord Jesus Christ in sincerity;
- when a church that is governed by its elders feels a unity with another church which is presided over by a bishop;
- when a certain church, although it holds with mutual edification and no formal preaching ministry, yet has no quarrel with those who love the centrality of teaching and exposition of the Word;
- when, in fact, we have agreed in this one thing, that we will search the Word independently and act out according to our light what we find to be true, but that, having done so, we will keep the unity of Spirit in the bond of peace.

I say this is most desirable and this it is that we are to seek after: not the fusion of all into one denomination, but the keeping of each church in its own distinct, independent testimony in love with every other church that is doing the same.

Now, in order to this, I have a few suggestions to offer. It is quite certain we shall never keep the unity of the Spirit if a church should declare that it is superior to every other. If there is a church which says, 'We are *the* church, and all others are mere sects; we are established, and others are only tolerated', then it is a troubler in Israel and must hide its head when the unity of the Spirit is so much as hinted at. Any church which lifts up its head on high and boasts over other churches has violated the unity of the Spirit. If other churches reply, 'One is our Master and we are all brethren', they do not violate the unity of the Spirit, for they simply claim their rights and speak the truth. That other church which forgets its true position as one in the family, and begins to set itself up as mistress and claim pre-eminence over its fellow servants, has put it out of its own power to keep the unity of the Spirit, for it has violated it once and for all.

A church that would keep the unity of the Spirit, again, must not consider itself to be so infallible that *not* to belong to its membership is sin. What right has any one church to set itself up as the standard, so that those who do not join it are necessarily Dissenters? It is true my Episcopal brother is a Dissenter, he dissents from me; it is true he is a Nonconformist, for he does not conform to me. I would not, however, call him by such names, lest I should arrogate to my own church to be the one church, and so should break the unity of the Spirit. If I turn to history, I may believe that my church can claim a long line of ancestors descending from the apostles, without ever running through the Church of Rome, but shall I therefore call a brother who does not quite see this succession a schismatic, and denominate his assembly a conventicle?[6] If he is a schismatic because he does not come to my place, why am I not a schismatic because I do not go to his? But he divides the church! He ought to come and worship with me. Ought I not to go and worship with him? But we are the larger number! Are divine things to be ruled by the majority? Where would the church of God be any day if it came to polling? I am afraid the devil would always be at the head of the poll. We wish to keep the unity of the Spirit, and if we have a little sister, we will treat her all the more kindly, owing to the fewness of her members.

If I want to 'keep the unity of the Spirit in the bond of peace', I must never call in the magistrate to force my brother to pay for washing my surplice, ringing my bell, and winding up my clock. I must not tell my brother that he is bound to pay for the support of my worship.[7] 'Oh!' he says, 'My dear friend, I pay for the maintenance of the worship which I believe to be correct, and I am quite willing that you should do the same for yours; I would voluntarily assist you if you were poor.' But you tell me you will put me in prison if I do not pay, and yet tell me to keep the unity of the Spirit. My dear friend, it is not keeping the unity of the Spirit to take away my stool and my table and my candlestick, and say you will put me in limbo, or haul me before an ecclesiastical court. You send the constable after me; and then if I say a word about it, you say, 'Charity hopes all things.' Yes, among the rest, it hopes that you will give up your sin in this matter.

If we should stand possessed of a piece of ground where we bury our dead, and if there should happen to come a member of another Christian church who would wish to lay his poor dead baby in our ground, there being no other convenient spot anywhere, and he asks the favour, I think we can hardly be thought to keep the unity of the Spirit if we tell him, 'No, nothing of the kind; you had your child sprinkled, therefore it cannot be buried with us Christians; we will not have your sprinkled baby lying alongside of our baptized dead.' I do not think that is keeping the unity of the Spirit. And I do not think when some churches have turned from their graveyard gate the mourners who have brought an unbaptized infant, and when the mourners have gone back weeping to their homes — I do not think such churches have been endeavouring to keep the unity of the Spirit in the bond of peace.

Again, if churches are to agree one with another, they must not make rules that ministers who are not of their own denomination shall not occupy their pulpits. I should be ashamed of you, if you passed a resolution that no one dissenting from us should stand in my pulpit. But we know a church which says, 'No matter how good a man may be — he may be a man as venerated as John Angell James[8] or he may have all the excellences of a William Jay[9] — we would not, perhaps, mind hearing him in a Town Hall, but into the sacredness of our particular rostrum these interlopers must not intrude.' 'For,' says this church, 'ours are ministers, yours are only lay-teachers. Ours are sacraments: the cup of blessing which we bless is the blood of Christ, and the bread which we break is the body of Christ; you have no sacramental efficacy with you. You are not a church in fact, but only a body of schismatics, meeting together to carry out what you think to be right. We tolerate you; that is all we can do.' Where is the unity of the Spirit there?

My dear friends, I received this text from one of the most holy men in the Church of England: if I expound it slightly for that church's benefit, he will, I trust, excuse me, for I do so in all honesty, desiring to aid him and many others in revision and reform. If this church were in the same condition as the Church of England, I would pray to be as plain in my remarks. I say it is an anachronism; it is a thing out of date for the nineteenth century, for any one church in this land, and that church the only one which defiles her hand by taking state-pay, to stand up and say, 'We are *the* Church; our ministers are *the* ministers; our people are *the* people; and now, dear brothers, shake hands, and endeavour to keep the unity of the Spirit of God.' Why, it is preposterous. Let us meet on equal ground; let us lay aside all pretences to superiority; let us really aid and not oppress each other; let us mingle in prayer; let us unite in confession of sin; let us join heartily in reforming our errors, and may a true Evangelical Alliance[10] cover our land. If any church will take the Bible as its standard and in the power of the Spirit of God preach the name of Jesus, there are thousands of us who will rejoice to give the right hand of fellowship with a hearty greeting to all such. We are every day striving to get other churches and ourselves more and more into that condition in which, while holding our own, we can yet keep the unity of the Spirit in the bond of peace.

The connection of one church member to another

Now I have a few words for you in regard to your relationship to one another as members of the same church. If we are to endeavour to keep the unity of the Spirit in the bond of peace in the same church, then we must avoid everything that would mar it.

Gossip — gossip is a very ready means of separating friends from one another. Let us endeavour to talk of something better than each other's characters. Dionysius (a Greek political leader) went down to the Academy to Plato;[11] Plato asked what he came for. 'Why,' said Dionysius, 'I thought that you, Plato, would be talking against me to your students.' Plato made this answer: 'Do you think, Dionysius, we are so destitute of matter to converse upon that we talk of you?' Truly we must be very short of subjects when we begin to talk of one another. It is better by far that we magnify Christ than detract from the honour of his members.

We must lay aside all *envy*. Multitudes of good people liked the Reformation, but they said they did not like the idea of its being done by a poor miserable monk, like Martin Luther. So there are many who like to see good things done, and good works carried on, but do not care to see it done by that upstart young brother, or that poor man, or that woman who has no particular rank or state. As a church let us shake off envyings; let us all rejoice in God's light.

And as for *pride* — if any of you have grown vainglorious of late, shake it off. I hope to exercise a ministry in this place which will drive out those of you who will not acknowledge your brethren when they are poorer or of less education than yourselves. What if the man does mar the Queen's English when he talks? What does that matter, so long as his heart is right? As long as you can feel he loves the Master, surely you can put up with his faults of language, if he can put up with your faults of action.

Then let us cultivate everything that would tend to unity. Are any sick? Let us care for them. Are any suffering? Let us weep with them. Do we know one who has less love than others? Then let us have more, so as to make up the deficiency. Do we perceive faults in a brother? Let us admonish him in love and affection. I pray you be peacemakers; everyone let the church go on in holy concord and blessed unity. Let us remember that we cannot keep the unity of the Spirit unless we all believe the truth of God. Let us search our Bibles, therefore, and conform our views and sentiments to the teaching of God's Word. I have already told you that unity in error is unity in ruin. We want unity in the truth of God through the Spirit of God. Let us seek this; let us live near to Christ, for this is the best way of promoting unity.

Divisions in churches never begin with those full of love to the Saviour. Cold hearts, unholy lives, inconsistent actions, neglected closets: these are the seeds which sow schisms in the body. But he who lives near to Jesus, wears his likeness, and copies his example, will be, wherever he goes, a sacred bond, a holy link to bind the church more closely together than ever.

May God give us this, and henceforth let us endeavour to keep the unity of the Spirit in the bond of peace. I commend the text to all believers to be practised through the coming days. And to those who are not believers, what can I say but that I trust their unity and their peace may be broken for ever, and that they may be led to Christ Jesus to find peace in his death. May faith be given, and then love and every grace will follow, so that they may be one with us in Christ Jesus our Lord. Amen.

The Word and the Spirit

Chapter 3

Pricked in the heart

May it ever be the preacher's one desire to win men to repentance towards God and faith in our Lord Jesus Christ! ... Oh, that we could so preach that our hearers should be at once pricked in their hearts, and so be led at once to believe in our Lord Jesus...

3.
Pricked in the heart

Therefore let all the house of Israel know assuredly, that God has made this Jesus, whom you crucified, both Lord and Christ. Now when they heard this, they were cut to the heart, and said to Peter and the rest of the apostles, 'Men and brethren, what shall we do?' — Acts 2:36-37

A sermon delivered on Lord's Day morning, 1 September 1889, by C. H. Spurgeon, at the Metropolitan Tabernacle, Newington. Sermon No. 2102

This was the first public preaching of the gospel after our Lord was taken up into glory. It was thus a very memorable sermon, a kind of first fruits of the great harvest of gospel testimony. It is very encouraging to those who are engaged in preaching that the first sermon should have been so successful. Three thousand made up a grand take of fish at that first cast of the net. We are serving a great and growing cause in the way chosen of God, and we hope in the future to see still larger results produced by that same undying and unchanging power which helped Peter to preach such a heart-piercing sermon.

Peter's discourse was not distinguished by any special rhetorical display; he did not use the words of man's wisdom or eloquence. It was not an oration; it was a heart-moving argument, entreaty, and exhortation. He gave his hearers a simple, well-reasoned, scriptural discourse, sustained by the facts of experience, and every passage of it pointed to the Lord Jesus. It was in these respects a model of what a sermon's contents ought to be. His plea was personally addressed to the people who stood before him, and it had a practical and pressing relation to them and to their conduct. It was aimed not at the head, but at the heart. Every word of it was directed to the conscience and the affections. It was plain, practical, personal, and persuasive; and in this it was a model of what a sermon's aim and style ought to be.

Yet Peter could not have spoken otherwise under the impression of the divine Spirit. His speech was as the oracles of God, a true product of a divine inspiration. Under the circumstances, any other kind of address would have been sadly out of place. A flashy, dazzling oration would have been a piece of horrible irreverence to the Holy Spirit, and Peter would have been guilty of the blood of souls if he had attempted it. In sober earnestness he kept to the plain facts of the case, setting them in the light of God's Word; and then with all his might he pressed home the truth upon those for whose salvation he was labouring. May it ever be the preacher's one desire to win men to repentance towards God and faith in our Lord Jesus Christ! May no minister wish to be admired, but may he long that his Lord and Master may be sought after! May none bewilder their people with the clouds of theoretic philosophy, but refresh them with the rain of revealed truth! Oh, that we could so preach that our hearers should be at once pricked in their hearts, and so be led at once to believe in our Lord Jesus, and immediately to come forward and confess their faith in his name!

We must not forget, however, to trace the special success of the sermon on the day of Pentecost to the outpouring of the Holy Spirit, in which Peter had shared. This is the making of the preacher. Immersed in the Holy Spirit, the preacher will think rightly and speak wisely; his word will be with power to those who hear. We must not forget, also, that there had been a long season of earnest, united, believing prayer on the part of the whole church. Peter was not alone. He was the voice of a praying company, and the believers had been with one accord in one place crying for a blessing; and thus not only was the Spirit resting upon the preacher, but on all who were with him.

What a difference this makes to a preacher of the gospel, when all his comrades are as much anointed of the Spirit as himself! His power is enhanced a hundred-fold. We shall seldom see the very greatest wonders wrought when the preacher stands by himself, but when Peter is described as standing up 'with the eleven', then there is a twelve-man ministry concentrated in one. When the inner circle is further sustained by a company of men and women who have entered into the same truth, and are of one heart and one soul, then the power is increased beyond measure.

A lonely ministry may sometimes effect great things, as Jonah did in Nineveh; but if we look for the greatest and most desirable result of all, it must come from one who is not alone but is the mouthpiece of many. Peter had the 120 registered brethren for a loving bodyguard, and this tended to make him strong for his Lord. How greatly I value the loving cooperation of the friends around me! I have no words to express my gratitude to God for the army of true men and women who surround me with their love and support me with their faith. I urge you, never cease to sustain me by your prayers, your sympathy, and your cooperation, until some other preacher shall take my place when increasing years shall warn me to stand aside.

Yet much responsibility must rest with the preacher himself, and there was much about Peter's own self that is well worthy of imitation. The sermon was born of the occasion, and it used the event of the hour as God intended it to be used. It was earnest without a trace of passion, and prudent without a suspicion of fear. The preacher himself was self-collected, calm, courteous, and gentle. He aired no theories, but went on firm ground, stepping from fact to fact, from Scripture to Scripture, from plain truth to plain truth. He was patient at the beginning, argumentative all along, and conclusive at the end. He fought his way through the doubts and prejudices of his hearers, and when he came to the end he stated the inevitable conclusion with clearness and certainty. All along he spoke very boldly, without mincing the truth: 'You have taken by lawless hands, have crucified, and put to death; whom God raised up' (Acts 2:23-24). He boldly accused them of the murder of the Lord of glory, doing his duty in the sight of God and for the good of their souls, with great firmness and fearlessness.

Yet there is great tenderness in his discourse. Impulsive and hot-headed Peter, who, a little while before, had drawn his sword to fight for his Lord, does not, in this instance, use a harsh word, but speaks with great gentleness and meekness of spirit, using words and terms all through the address which indicate a desire to conciliate, and then to convince. Though he was as faithful as an Elijah, yet he used terms so courteous and kindly that, if men took offence, it would not be because of any offensiveness of tone on the speaker's part. Peter was gentle in his manner, but forceful in his matter. This art he had learned from his Lord, and we shall never have master-preachers among us till we see men who have been with Jesus, and have learned of him.

Oh, that we could become partakers of our Lord's spirit, and echoes of his tone! Then may we hope to attain to Pentecostal results, when we have preachers like Peter, surrounded by a band of earnest witnesses, and all baptized with the Holy Spirit and with fire.

When we follow the run of Peter's argument, we do not wonder that his hearers were pricked in their hearts. We ascribe that deep compunction to the Spirit of God, and yet it was a very reasonable thing that it should be so. When it was clearly shown to them that they had really crucified the Messiah, the great hope of their nation, it was not surprising that they should be smitten with horror. Looking as they were for Israel's King, and finding that he had been among them, and they had despitefully used him, and crucified him, they might well be smitten at the heart.

Though for the result of our ministry we depend wholly upon the Spirit of God, yet we must adapt our discourse to the end we aim at; or, say rather, we must leave ourselves in the Spirit's hand as to the sermon itself as well as in reference to the result of the sermon. The Holy Spirit uses means which are adapted to the end designed. Because, beloved, I do desire beyond all things that many may be pricked in the heart, I have taken this concluding part of Peter's discourse to be the text of this sermon. Yet my trust is not in the Word itself, but in the quickening Spirit who works by it. May the Spirit of God use the rapier of his Word to pierce the hearts of my readers!

First, note that Peter speaks to his hearers upon their evil conduct to the Lord Jesus; and, secondly, he declares to them the exaltation that God had bestowed upon Jesus. When we have dwelt on these two things, we will notice, in the third place, the result of knowing this grand fact: 'Let all the house of Israel know assuredly, that God has made this Jesus, whom you crucified, both Lord and Christ.'

1. Evil conduct towards the Lord Jesus

First, then, Peter dwelt tenderly, but very plainly, upon their evil conduct towards the Lord Jesus. 'He came to his own, and his own did not receive him' (John 1:11). As a nation, Israel had rejected him whom God had sent. The inhabitants of Jerusalem had gone further, and had consented to his death; they had even clamoured for it, crying, 'Crucify him, crucify him!' (Luke 23:21). Solemnly the Jews had exclaimed, 'His blood be on us and on our children' (Matt. 27:25). None of them had protested against the murder of the innocent One, but many of them had been eager to make an end of him. In plain words, Peter charged this upon them, and they could not deny it; nor did they pretend to do so. It is well when a sense of guilt compels a man to stand silent under the rebuke of God. We then have hope of him that he will seek for pardon.

Men and brethren, we are not in Jerusalem, and the death of our Lord happened more than eighteen hundred years ago; therefore we need not dwell upon the sin of those long since dead. It will be more profitable for us practically to consider how far we have been guilty of similar sins against the Lord Jesus Christ. Let us look at home. Let each one consider his own case.

The sin of blasphemy

I may be addressing some today who have blasphemed the name of the Lord Jesus. I do not suppose that you have been guilty of the vulgar language of blasphemy, which is coarse and revolting as well as profane, but there are politer methods of committing the same crime. Some, with their elaborate criticisms of Christianity, wound it far more seriously than do atheists with their profanities. In these days, wiseacres, with their philosophy, derogate from the glory of our Lord's nature, and, with their novel doctrines, undermine his gospel. Denying the atonement, or teaching it as something other than a substitutionary sacrifice, they try to make away with that which is the very heart and soul of the Redeemer's work. Men nowadays drink in opinions which lessen the guilt of sin, and, of course, lower the value of the atoning blood. The cross is still a stone of stumbling and a rock of offence.

Men do not now accept the words of the Bible as authoritative, nor the teaching of the apostles as final; they set themselves up to be teachers of the great Teacher, reformers of the divine gospel. They do not accept the teaching of the Lord Jesus one half so much as they criticize it. If any of you have been guilty of this, may the Holy Spirit convict you of your sin!

Since the Lord God has made this atoning Jesus both Lord and Christ, and set him on his right hand, any teaching which does despite to him — however learned, however advanced, however cultured it may seem to be — is a grievous sin against the Lord God himself. By such conduct we are, as far as in us lies, again putting the Lord Jesus to death; we are attempting to make away with that which is the very life and glory of Christ. Oh, if you have denied his deity, rejected his atoning blood, ridiculed his imputed righteousness, or scoffed at salvation by faith in him, may you be pricked in the heart as you see that God has made that same Jesus to be Lord of all!

The sin of ignoring the claims of Christ

Much more common, however, is another sin against our Lord Jesus — namely, neglecting him, ignoring his claims, and postponing the day of faith in him. I trust that none of you are willing to die unconverted, or would even dare to think of passing away without being washed in the precious blood; yet you have lived to manhood, to ripe years, perhaps even to old age, without yielding your hearts to the Lord Jesus and accepting him as your Saviour.

To say the least of it, this is a very sad piece of neglect. To ignore a man altogether is, in a certain sense, as far as you are concerned, to kill that man. If you put him out of your reckoning, if you treat him as if he were nothing, if your estimate of his life is made as if he were a cipher, you have put your Lord out of existence in reference to yourself. You treat him with empty compliment by observing his day, and hearing his Word, but you have no real regard for him. Is this not a cruel fault? From morning till night your Lord is not in all your thoughts; he never affects your dealings with your fellow men; you never endeavour to catch his spirit of love and considerateness and meekness; and thus, as a leader and exemplar, he is dead to you.

You have never confessed your sin before him, nor sought for pardon at his hands, nor have you looked to see whether he has borne your sins in his own body on the tree. Oh, soul, this is base neglect — ungrateful contempt! God thinks so much of his Son that he cannot set him too high; he has placed him at his own right hand, and yet you will not spare him a thought! The great God thinks heaven and earth too little for him, and magnifies him exceedingly above all, as King of kings and Lord of lords; and yet you treat him as if he were of no account, and might be safely made to wait your time and leisure. Is this right? Will you treat your Saviour this way? May this prick you in the heart, and may you cease from this base ingratitude!

The sin of rejecting Christ

There are others who have done more than this, for they have rejected Christ. I now allude to those of you who have not been able to resist the appeals made to you by the Lord's ministers. You have felt a good deal more than you would like to confess. You have been so inclined to seek the Saviour that you have almost done so; sin has flashed in your face like the flames of Tophet, and in alarm you have resolved to seek salvation. You have gone home to bend the knee in prayer; you have read the Scriptures to learn the way of eternal life; but, alas! An evil companion crossed your path, and the question came, 'Shall it be this man or Christ?' You chose the man — I had almost said, you chose Barabbas — and rejected Jesus. A sinful pleasure came before you when you had begun to be serious, and the question arose, 'Shall I give up this pleasure, or shall I renounce all hope of Christ?' You snatched at the pleasure, and you let your Saviour go. Do you not remember when you did violence to your conscience? There was an effort about it as you stifled conviction. You had to put forth a decided act of the will to quench the Spirit of God, and to escape from the strivings of your awakened conscience.

I do not know to whom this may apply, but I am certain, as certain as Peter was when he spoke to the crucifiers of Christ, that I am speaking to some who have been rejecters of the Lord Jesus Christ, not once nor twice. Some of you have distinctly rejected him almost every Lord's Day, especially when the Word of the Lord has been proclaimed with extraordinary power, and you have felt it shake you, as a lion shakes his prey. Thank God, you are not past feeling yet!

I urge you, do not presume upon the continuance of your tenderness. You will not always feel as you have felt. The day may come when even the thunders of God may not be heard by your deafened ear, and the love of Christ will not affect the heart which you have made callous by wilful obstinacy. Woe to the man when his heart is turned to stone! When flesh turns to stone, it is a conversion unto eternal death, just as the turning of stone to flesh is conversion to eternal life. May God have mercy upon you, and prick you in the heart today, while you yet have tenderness enough to feel that you have rejected him whom you ought to embrace with all your heart!

The sin of forsaking Jesus Christ

I must come a little closer to certain of you, who have forsaken the Lord Jesus Christ. There are a few unhappy people over whom I greatly grieve because of their wanderings; and yet I am glad that they have not quite forsaken the courts of the Lord's house. These once professed to be disciples of Christ, but they have gone back, and walk no more with him. They were once numbered with us, and went in and out of our solemn assemblies for prayer and breaking of bread, but now we do not know them. They were not backward to confess themselves Christians, but now they deny their Lord. In former days they were zealous and apparently devout; they were quick in the service of God and sound in their creed.

But there came a day — I need not describe the circumstances, for they differ in different cases — when two roads were before them, and they must go either to the right or to the left; and they took the road by which they turned their back upon Christ and upon the vitality of godliness. They went off into sin, and apostatized from the faith. We fear 'They went out from us, but they were not of us; for if they had been of us, they would have continued with us' (1 John 2:19). They have gone aside to crooked ways and we fear that the Lord will lead them forth with the workers of iniquity. Oh, backslider, I hope you are not a Judas; my trust is that you may be a Peter! You have denied your Master, but I hope you will yet weep bitterly, and be restored to your Lord's service. For your good I must bring home your wanderings to you; may the Lord prick you in the heart about them! Why have you left your Lord? Wherein has he wearied you?

There may be those who were once glad to be numbered with the children of God, but now they care nothing for God or his people. Alas! They take part with the adversaries of Christ and the despisers of his precious blood!

Friend, I must bring your sin to remembrance and ask you why you have done this thing! Were you a hypocrite? If not, why have you turned aside? God has exalted to his throne the Saviour, on whom you have turned your back. Have you not acted madly in what you have done? The Most High God is on the side of Jesus, and you are avowedly on the other side. Is this right, or wise? It is painful to me to speak of these things. I hope it is far more painful for you to read them. I want you to feel as David did when his heart smote him. What have you been doing? Has the Lord Jesus deserved this at your hands? Turn, I urge you, from your evil way, and turn unto the Lord with full purpose of heart.

2. Jesus exalted by God

After Peter had dwelt upon the sin of his hearers in treating the Lord so ill, he declared to them the exaltation bestowed on him by God. The great God loved and honoured and exalted that same Jesus whom they had crucified. Whatever you may think of the Lord Jesus, God thinks everything of him! To you he may be dead and buried, but God has raised him from the dead. To God he is the ever-living, the ever well-beloved Christ. You cannot destroy the Lord Jesus or his cause. If you could do all that the most malicious heart could suggest, you could not really defeat him. Men wreaked their vengeance on him once: they put him to a felon's death, they laid him in the grave, and sealed the stone; but he rose again, for God was on his side.

Whatever you do you cannot shake the truth of the gospel, nor rob the Lord Jesus of a single beam of his glory. He lives and reigns and he will live and reign, whatever becomes of you. You may refuse his salvation, but he is still a Saviour, and a great one. His gospel chariot rolls on, and every stone that is placed to hinder it is crushed into the earth, and compelled to make a road for him. If you resist the Lord, you do it at your peril, but you do it in vain. You might as well hope to reverse the laws of nature, quench the sun, and snatch the moon from its orbit, as hope to overthrow the cause and kingdom of the Lord Jesus; for God is on his side, and his throne is established forever.

God has raised his Son from the dead, and taken him up to sit at his right hand, and there he will remain while his enemies shall be made his footstool. By this you may see what evil you have done through rejecting Christ, and may know who he is whom you have neglected, refused, and forsaken.

Infinite gladness at God's right hand

Let me remind you that, when we read of our Lord as being at the right hand of God, we perceive that he enjoys infinite felicity. At the right hand of God there are pleasures for evermore; and David said, as the representative of our Lord, 'You have made known to me the ways of life; you will make me full of joy in your presence' (Acts 2:28). He who was the man of sorrows now overflows with gladness. All his work and warfare done, he rests in boundless blessedness. His priestly work being finished, he sits down. No more does he feel the cross and nails, no more does he endure the mockery of cruel eyes and ribald lips. He is full of joy, that joy which he bids his people share when he says, 'Enter into the joy of your Lord' (Matt. 25:21). His portion is measureless, infinite, inconceivable delight.

Can it be that you are opposed to him and neglect him, while God lavishes upon him more than all the bliss of heaven, and makes him to be the fountain of unspeakable delight to all his redeemed ones? Grieve that you should grieve him whom God thus loads with blessedness.

Infinite majesty at God's right hand

Moreover, remember that at the right hand of God our Lord sits in infinite majesty. Jesus — whom you think little of, Jesus — from whom you turn aside, is today adored by angels, obeyed by seraphs, worshipped by just men made perfect. He is the highest in the highest heavens. Do you not hear the blast of heaven's trumpets, which proclaims him head over principalities and powers? Do you not hear the song which ascribes to him honour, and glory, and power, and dominion, and might?

My faith anticipates the happy day when I shall stand a courtier in his unrivalled courts and behold him, the Lamb upon the throne, reigning high over all, with every knee in heaven and in earth gladly bowing before him. Can it be that you have neglected him whom God has exalted? Can it be that you have refused him, that you have shown contempt towards him, that you have, as far as you could, put to death him whom Jehovah has made Lord of all?

Seated in the place of power

Nor is this all, for the place at the right hand of God, to which he is now exalted, is the place of power. There sits the Mediator, the Son of God, the man Christ Jesus, while his enemies are being subdued under him. Do not believe, oh proudest of doubters, that you can take away from Christ any measure of his power! He overrules all mortal things; he directs the movements of the stars; he rules the armies of heaven. He restrains the rage of his adversaries, and what he suffers to be let loose he turns to his glory. All power is given to him in heaven and earth; he reigns in the three realms of nature, providence, and grace. His kingdom rules over all, and of his dominion there shall be no end. What do our hearts suggest but that we bow at his feet, that we worship him with loving reverence, that we yield to that supreme power which is used for purposes of love? Yet it is this Christ, this mighty Christ, who is despised by some of you, so that you run the risk of perishing because you have no heart for him and his great salvation.

Seated as Judge

Learn, next, that he is at the right hand of the Majesty in the heavens, seated as our Judge. If we refuse him as a Saviour, we shall not be able to escape from him as Judge in the last great day. All the acts of men are being recorded, and in that day, when the great white throne shall be set in the heavens, all things shall be made manifest, and we must stand unveiled in his presence.

You have often heard and sung of him whose face was more marred than that of any man, when he was here as a sacrifice for guilty men. If you refuse him, you will have to stand before his bar to answer for it. The most awful sight for the impenitent in the day of judgement will be the face of the Lord Jesus Christ. I do not find that they cry, 'Hide us from the tempest', nor 'Hide us from the angel-guards', nor 'Hide us from their swords of fire', but, 'Hide us from the face of him who sits on the throne and from the wrath of the Lamb' (Rev. 6:16). Love, when once it turns to wrath, is terrible beyond compare. As oil when set on fire blazes with great force, so the meek and loving Jesus, when finally rejected, will exhibit a wrath more terrible than death.

> You sinners, seek his grace, whose wrath you cannot bear;
> Fly to the shelter of his cross, and find salvation there.

Perhaps through ignorance you have rebelled; repent, and take another course. You supposed that when you kicked against a sermon, you had only put down the minister's words, but in reality you resisted the Saviour's love. You thought that when you turned away from Christ and his people, it was only leaving a church, and having your name crossed out of a book. Ah! Take heed, for I fear you have left the Lamb of God, and renounced your part in his Book of Life! At the last it may turn out to have been an awful thing to have been put forth from the church of Christ on earth; for when we, as a church, do our Lord's bidding, that which we bind on earth is bound in heaven. In refusing the Lord's Word, you refuse him who speaks from heaven. You refuse not only his words, but himself, and he shall be your Judge — your Judge most just, most holy. Oh, how will you bear it? How will you bear to stand at the bar of the despised Saviour?

Head over all things for his church

Peter also showed his hearers that the Lord was greatly exalted in heaven as the Head over all things to his church, for he had that day shed abroad the Holy Spirit. When the Holy Spirit comes, he comes from Christ and as the witness of his power. He proceeds from the Father and the Son, and he bears witness with both. Christ's power was marvellously proved when, after he had been only a little while in heaven, he was able to bestow such gifts upon men, and specially to send the tongues of fire and the rushing mighty wind, which are signs of the energy of the Holy Spirit.

He is such a Lord that he can save or destroy. The Christ that died upon the cross has all things committed into his hands. He can at this moment send forth salvation to the ends of the earth, so that multitudes shall believe and live, for God has exalted him with his right hand to be a Prince and a Saviour, to give repentance and forgiveness of sins. Or, he can turn the key the other way, and shut the door against this untoward generation; for what he opens, no man shuts; and what he shuts, no man opens. In any case, be sure of this, you Gentiles, even as Peter would have the house of Israel be sure of it, that 'God has made that same Jesus, whom you have crucified, both Lord and Christ.'

I notice that few writers or preachers use the expression, 'our Lord Jesus Christ'. We have 'lives of Christ' and 'lives of Jesus', but brothers, he is THE LORD. Jesus is both Lord and Christ. We need to acknowledge his deity, his dominion, and his divine anointing. He is 'God over all, blessed forever', and we can never praise him too much. A great and grievous error of the times is a lack of reverence for our Lord and his sacrifice. To sit in judgement on his sacred teaching is to spit in his face; to deny his miracles is to strip him of his own clothes; to make him out to be a mere teacher of ethics is to mock him with a purple robe; and to deny his atonement, in philosophical phraseology, is to crown him with thorns, and crucify him afresh, and put him to an open shame. Do not be guilty of this, for God has made this same Jesus 'both Lord and Christ'; let us worship him as Lord, and trust him as Christ.

3. The result of knowing Jesus as both Lord and Christ

Now I come to my closing point, which is the result of knowing this assuredly. May I pause to ask, 'Do you know this assuredly?' I hope all of you believe that God has made Jesus Christ, the Mediator, in his complex person, as God-and-man, to be 'both Lord and Christ'. He was Lord, as God, always; but as God-and-man, he is now Lord and Christ. Manhood and Godhead are united in him in one wondrous person, and this person is 'both Lord and Christ'. You believe it. But do you so believe it that it is a fact of the utmost importance to you? Will you truly believe that the man of Nazareth, who died on Calvary, is both Lord and Christ?

If you do now believe this, what are your feelings as you review your past misconduct towards him? Does not your past neglect prick you in the heart? If you do not so believe, it is of little use for me to describe what the result of such belief would be, for that result will not take place in you.

But if you have so believed, and Jesus is to you Lord and Christ, you will look on him whom you have pierced and mourn for him. As you recollect your negligence of him, your rejection of him, your backsliding from him, and all your ungrateful acts which show contempt of him, your heart will be ready to break, and you will be seized with a great sorrow, and a hearty repentance. May the Lord work it in you, for his Son's sake!

Souls pierced by truth

Observe, that as the result of Peter's sermon, his hearers felt a mortal sting: 'They were cut to the heart.' The truth had pierced their souls. When a man finds out that he has done a fearful wrong to one who loved him, he grows sick at heart, and views his own conduct with abhorrence.

Remember the story of Llewellyn[1] and his faithful dog: The prince came back from the hunt and missed his infant child, but saw marks of blood everywhere. Suspecting his dog Gelert of having killed the child, he drove his vengeful sword into the faithful hound, which had been bravely defending his child against a huge wolf, which lay there, all torn and dead, 'tremendous still in death'. Yes, he had slain the faithful creature which had preserved his child. Poor Gelert's dying yell pierced the prince to the heart, and well it might. If such emotions fitly arise when we discover that we have, in error, been ungenerous and cruel to a dog, how ought we to feel towards the Lord Jesus, who laid down his life that we, who were his enemies, might live?

I recall an awfully tragic story of an evil couple who kept an inn of low repute. A young man called one night to lodge. They noticed that he had gold in his purse, and they murdered him in the night. It was their own son, who had come back to gladden their old age, and wished to see whether his parents would remember him. Oh, the bitterness of their lamentation when they found that through the lust of gold they had murdered their own son! Take out of such amazing grief its better portion, and then add to it a spiritual conviction of the sin of evil-entreating the Son of God, the perfect One, the Lover of our souls, and you come near the meaning of being 'cut to the heart'. Oh, to think that we should despise him who loved us and gave himself for us, and should rebel against him who bought us with his own blood while we were his enemies! I would to God everyone that has not come to Christ would feel a sting in his conscience now, and would mourn that he has done this exceeding evil thing against the ever-blessed Son of God, who became man and died for love of guilty men.

Hearts moved with love

When we read 'They were cut to the heart,' we may see in it the meaning that they felt a movement of love to him — a relenting of heart, a stirring of emotion towards him. They said to themselves, 'Have we treated him this way? What can we do to show our horror of our own conduct?' They were not merely convinced of their fault so as to be grieved, but their desires and affections went out towards the offended one, and they cried, 'What shall we do? In what way can we acknowledge our wrong? Is there any way of undoing this ill towards him whom we now love?' I would have you all come to this point. I would have you know the meaning of Newton's[2] hymn:

I saw one hanging on a tree,
In agonies and blood,
Who fix'd his languid eyes on me,
As near his cross I stood

Sure never till my latest breath,
Can I forget that look;
It seem'd to charge me with his death,
Though not a word he spoke

My conscience felt and own'd the guilt,
And plunged me in despair;
I saw my sins his blood had spilt,
And help'd to nail him there

Alas! I knew not what I did;
But now my tears are vain;

Where shall my trembling soul be hid?
For I the Lord have slain.

Let us tearfully enquire how we can end our opposition, and prove ourselves to be his friends and humble servants.

Lives of obedient faith

As a consequence of Peter's sermon, preached in the power of the Holy Spirit, these people exhibited obedient faith. They were roused to action, and they said, 'Men and brethren, what shall we do?' They believed that the same Jesus whom they had crucified was now Lord of all, and they hastened to be obedient unto him. When Peter said, 'Repent!' they did indeed repent. If repentance is grief, they grieved at their hearts. If repentance is a change of mind and life, they were indeed altered men.

Then Peter said, 'Let every one of you be baptized in the name of Jesus Christ for the remission of sins.' Take the open and decisive step: stand forth as believers in Jesus, and confess him by that outward and visible sign which he has ordained. Be buried with him in whom your sin is buried. You slew him in error; be buried with him in truth. They did it gladly, they repented of the sin; they were baptized into the sacred name.

And then Peter could tell them, 'You have remission of sins. The wrong you have done to your Lord is cancelled; the Lord has put away your sin forever. Remission of sins comes to you through Jesus, whom you slew, whom the Father has raised up. You shall not be summoned before the bar of God to account even for the hideous crime of murdering the Lord, for by his death you are forgiven. In proof of forgiveness you shall now be made partakers of the great gift which marks his ascending power. The Holy Spirit shall come upon you, even upon you his murderers, and you shall go forth, and be witnesses for him.'

Oh, to what a place I have brought you! If indeed the Holy Spirit has helped you to follow me in my discourse, see where we have climbed! However black your crime, however vile your character, if you have seen the wrong that you have done, if you have repented of having done it because you see that you have sinned against your loving Lord, and if you will now come to him repenting and believing, and will confess him as he bids you confess him in baptism; then you have full remission, and you shall be partakers of the gifts and graces of his Holy Spirit, and henceforth you shall be chosen witnesses for the Christ whom God has raised from the dead. Beloved, you need no choice speech from me: pure gold needs no gilding, and as I have told you the most wonderful of all facts in heaven or in earth, I let it remain in all its simple grandeur.

May God write out this old, old story on your hearts! Oh, that he would issue a new edition of his gospel of love printed on your hearts! Every man's conversion is a freshly printed copy of the poem of salvation. May the Lord issue you hot from the press today, a living epistle to be known and read by all men, and specially to be read by your children at home and your neighbours in the same street! The Lord grant that hearts may be pricked by this sermon, for his name's sake! Amen.

The Word and the Spirit

Chapter 4

A voice with four messages

There is a temptation which assails all of us who preach to want to do some great thing. We fancy that if we could preach such a famous sermon as Jonathan Edwards delivered when he spoke of 'sinners in the hand of an angry God' ... then we should have lived to some purpose.

4.
A voice with four messages

Then he said, 'Go out, and stand on the mountain before the LORD.' And behold, the LORD passed by, and a great and strong wind tore into the mountains and broke the rocks in pieces before the LORD, but the LORD was not in the wind; and after the wind an earthquake, but the LORD was not in the earthquake; and after the earthquake a fire, but the LORD was not in the fire; and after the fire a still small voice. So it was, when Elijah heard it, that he wrapped his face in his mantle and went out and stood in the entrance of the cave. Suddenly a voice came to him, and said, 'What are you doing here, Elijah?' — 1 Kings 19:11-13

A sermon delivered on Thursday evening, 31 July 1873, by C. H. Spurgeon, published on Thursday, 18 November 1909. Sermon No. 3171

There may be a great deal more teaching in what Elijah saw and heard in the cave than I shall be able to bring out in one sermon. Indeed, I shall not attempt to exhaust the very wonderful, practical sermon which was preached to the prophet on the side of Mount Horeb, but in the still small voice I hear four messages.

1. A message to Elijah

First, there was a message to Elijah himself. He had, apparently, conceived the idea that the whole nation of Israel would be converted from idolatry by one grand display of divine power. If it could once be indisputably proved that Baal was not God, and that Jehovah alone was God, then he thought that surely the people would be convinced, and would loyally return to their old covenant with the one living and true God; but he found that it was not so.

Although the fire of the Lord had fallen from heaven and had consumed Elijah's sacrifice, burned up the very stones of the altar, and licked up the water in the trench, and although the people had cried out, 'Jehovah is God! Jehovah is God!', yet for all that they did not forsake Baal, nor the other idols that had been set up in the groves and on the high places; still the sun-god was worshipped and the God who made the sun was forgotten.

Elijah seems also to have thought that a display of terrible severity was necessary to bring these people back to their allegiance to Jehovah. Hence he took the prophets of Baal and the prophets of the groves, and put them to death at the brook Kishon, not permitting any one of them to escape. It must have been stern work for him to be the executioner of God's justice, but he did it with a sacred zest, feeling that he was only slaying those who were the enemies of God, and that every blow he struck at those idolatrous priests was struck for the honour and glory of Jehovah.

Yet that stern severity did not succeed as Elijah had expected it would, and one result of it was that Jezebel sent to threaten him with death. I think that possibly Elijah desired that God would inflict upon the people some still severer judgement; yet I know not what calamities he would have had them suffer, for there had already been dire distress through the three years of drought; even this had not driven the people from their idolatry.

Perhaps Elijah would have had fire and sword sent among them, to drive them from their idols and bring them back to the worship of Jehovah.

But God here teaches Elijah that this is not his way of working. He does use the wind and the earthquake and the fire when he pleases, but these are not his most effective instruments. He does not do his mightiest works by them, but in quite another way, by a still small voice. Thus the Lord practically said to Elijah, 'Gentler means must be tried with these rebellious people. My glory will be promoted among them by other methods than you have yet used, or than I have used by you as my servant. I have let them see that I am Lord and Master of the terrible forces of nature, I have convinced them that I am a great God who can smite them as much as I please, but I have not thereby won their hearts; there must be other methods used. The still small voice must be tried.'

You have, perhaps, noticed that Elijah's later ministry — although it still remained one of fire, and although his was still the voice that cried in the wilderness as John the Baptist's was to do later, 'Make straight in the desert a highway for our God' — became, on the whole, much more gentle and tender. He seems to have devoted himself to the work of perpetuating the ministry among the people by founding schools of the prophet, for the young men, who are called the sons of the prophets, evidently recognized him as their master and head, as they recognized Elisha after Elijah had been carried up to heaven.

The still small voice of prophetic teaching was to be tried. Judgements had apparently failed, for the hard hearts of the people had not been softened and subdued. Men had been terrified, but they had not been converted. They had been frightened out of their sins for a time, but they had speedily returned to them, as swine that might be washed would soon be again wallowing in the mire. Satan had been dislodged from them for a little while, but he had returned, and brought other devils with him, and so made his possession of them the more secure. Now other methods were to be tried, gentler, softer, quieter methods, which would prove to be more efficient. I think that was the message of God to Elijah through the still small voice.

2. A message to all God's ministers

Secondly, if I understand that voice correctly, there was a message in it to all God's ministers. To all of us who preach the Word, or who try to teach it in any way, God seems to say, 'Do not trust in great displays of force, in tremendous demonstrations of power; trust rather in the still soft influences of the distilling dew of God's Spirit and the gentle rain of the gospel. Preach the Word to the sons and daughters of men.'

There is a temptation which assails all of us who preach to want to do some great thing. We fancy that if we could preach such a famous sermon as Jonathan Edwards[1] delivered when he spoke of 'sinners in the hands of an angry God', when the people felt as though the very seats upon which they sat moved under them, and some of them even stood up and grasped the pillars of the building in their terror — we fancy that if only we could preach in such a style as that, then we should have lived to some purpose.

Or we think that, if we had the eloquence of Whitefield[2] and could go and stand, as he did, on Kennington Common, and preach to 20,000 people at a time, then we should have accomplished something worthy of our highest ambition.

Or it may be that we have some famous sermons of which we think a good deal. Possibly there is a fine peroration, like the grand finale of the Crystal Palace[3] fireworks; or there may be a great display of oratory all through the discourse.

Or if we have been wise enough to leave out all that sort of thing, we may have tried to make the sermon one that would convince the judgement of our hearers, or force its way into their understandings by its sheer sledgehammer power; and we have hoped, by preaching this way, to see our congregations converted.

Now, if we have been long in the ministry, and if the Lord has given us true spiritual understanding, we must have discovered how futile are all such hopes and expectations. There may be a great wind blowing while we are preaching such sermons, but the Lord is not in the wind. There may be a great earthquake, and the people may shake and quake with terror, but the Lord is not in the earthquake. Our pulpit may be lurid with the fire of coming judgement, but the Lord is not in the fire. It is true that we are to preach the terror of the Lord, but, like Paul, because we know the terror of the Lord, we are to 'persuade men' (2 Cor. 5:11). Persuasiveness is to be one of the dominant notes in our preaching just because of the terrible side of truth. We are not to conceal the threatenings that we find in the Word of God, for the gentle, loving Saviour uttered very terrible words concerning the wrath to come, the worm that never dies, and the fire that never can be quenched.

At the same time, our main reliance must not be on that style of preaching, and our expectation of blessing must not depend upon our heaping up words full of alarm and terror and expressions intended to set forth the woes and horrors of impending judgement; for, after all, we may alarm our hearers until they can be no longer alarmed, and we may make them weep in terror until they can weep no more; but, instead of doing so, they may even scoff at that which once so greatly disturbed them.

But the preaching of Jesus Christ and him crucified never loses its power. The telling over and over again of

> The old, old story
> Of Jesus and his love

never becomes a mere repetition, if with warm heart and loving spirit we still cry to our hearers, 'Behold the Lamb of God, who takes away the sin of the world' (John 1:29). There may be no excitement in our congregation, no sensation may be created by our preaching, but the Lord will be in it. He always has been in such preaching as that, and he always will be. A preached Saviour must mean saved sinners before long, but even where sinners are not saved, if we faithfully, lovingly, and earnestly preach the gospel to them, we are to God a sweet savour of Christ in those that perish as well as in those that are saved.

So let us still be content to go on and on and on and on preaching Jesus Christ, praying for the Spirit of God to rest upon us while we tell over and over and over again how the Son of God loved us, and gave himself for us; asking the faithful to pray that God will bless the Word; seeking to make our own lives more like the life of him whom we preach; and trying by all lawful means to be the instruments that God will bless in saving at least some of our hearers.

And we will succeed in such a ministry as this if we have faith in God, and faith in the message we are sent to deliver, for the Lord is still in the ministry of the still small voice. There have been many kinds of ministries in this world, but where has God ever been except in the ministry of the truth as it is in Jesus? There have been ministries of learning, and ministries of eloquence, and ministries of philosophy, and ministries that have made a fair show in the flesh; but, as a general rule, souls have not been saved by them.

The true soul-winning ministries are the ministries of the still small voice, the ministries that proclaim the redeeming grace and dying love of Jesus; and where those ministries are exercised, seeking souls will recognize the voice of God, and give heed to it. So there was a message in the still small voice to every preacher of the Word.

3. A message to the whole church of God

I think there was also, in that still small voice, a message to the whole church of God. The Lord was not in the wind, nor in the fire, nor in the earthquake; but he was in the still small voice.

Let us learn from this fact not to desire to see any great judgements fall upon any country, nor to see any extraordinary displays of divine power abroad in the world, with the idea that thereby God's kingdom will come. We sometimes grow dissatisfied because God's cause is not advancing as fast as we think it ought to advance. Foreign missions are not so successful as we should like to see them, and home missions do not prosper as we think they should. Then we recollect the times when the cholera[4] was rife in London and, remembering that the people seemed to be more tender in spirit then, and more willing to listen to the gospel, we have almost wished that some such visitation as that would come again to arouse the callous inhabitants of this sinful city and nation. Yet we must not cherish such a wish as that; for, after all, the good that comes in that way is more apparent than real, and, after the apparent softening, there often comes a hardening of the heart against the truth.

We have sometimes looked upon the nations of the earth, and as we have seen them infatuated with idolatry and given up to gross error, we have wondered, if war broke out, or pestilence, or there was some other form of the rod of God, whether there might not then be fresh doors opened for the preaching of the Word, and whether the people might not be more willing to listen to it when it was preached. It has, no doubt, been so in certain cases in the past, but let us not, even in our hearts, ever desire such calamities and chastisements to happen.

Let us still place our confidence where the confidence of the early Christian church was placed — in the Spirit of God working through the preaching of the gospel by earnest, faithful men who had themselves proved its power in their own hearts and lives.

A further lesson to the Lord's people, in the still small voice, is this: It appears, from what God said to Elijah, that there was a work going on in Israel of which the prophet knew nothing. There were 7,000 people whose knees had never been bent in the worship of the sun-god, and whose lips had never kissed the idol.

It is doubtless true today that there are thousands, of whom we know nothing, who are not partakers in the idolatry which causes us such sorrow of heart. What a cursed thing it is that idolatry of various kinds is so rampant today in this and other lands! Oh, God of Elijah, quickly put an end to it, we implore you! Yet, all the while that vile idolatry was spreading in Israel, the worship of the true God was being retained by 7,000 faithful souls, though Elijah did not know that there was even one beside himself.

How were they won to Jehovah? Certainly not by Elijah's impressive demonstration on the top of Carmel, for they were loyal to the Lord before that. Possibly, they were not converted even by the three years' drought; what then had made them so different from the bulk of their fellow countrymen? The secret movement of the Spirit of God upon their hearts; perhaps also the loving teaching of mothers by the fireside, the gracious influence of godly men and women upon their companions, and of the worshippers of Jehovah upon men of the world, who saw in them what they knew they did not possess themselves, and who so admired it that they enquired how they also might obtain such beauty of character — all these things had helped to range these 7,000 idol-haters on the side of Jehovah. The still small voice had been doing for Israel what Elijah could not do.

Brothers, a similar process is going on now, and I want to refresh your memories concerning it. Sometimes, as we carefully examine the organized Christianity of the present day, we cannot discover any progress at all. It is a great pity, and a cause for great sorrow, that there should not be any visible progress; but for all that, let us hope that there is an underground work going on, a secret work of God's grace proceeding in the hearts and lives of those by whom we are surrounded, although we can see no signs of it. You who put leaven in your bread know that you do not hear it making a noise during the night, but the leaven is working effectually although it is working silently.

There is still an open Bible in our land, and in many other lands beside, and so long as that is the case, you need not fear that Protestantism will die out, or that the lamp of truth will be put out.

There is also more than an open Bible in this and other lands; there are many praying people, who will take no rest and give God no rest until they see his cause and kingdom prospering in the earth. You may not know them, and they may not be among the great ones of this world, but there are many who are crying day and night to God for the preservation and the spread of his truth. There are eyes that are weeping over sin, and there are hearts that are nearly breaking for the longing that they have for the coming of the Redeemer's kingdom. There are people whose names will never be known to fame, some of the very poorest on the earth, who nevertheless are speaking softly with their voices for Jesus, and who are also speaking very powerfully by their lives for Jesus, as servants in the household, as toilers in the workshop, as poor humble bedridden sufferers who patiently endure great pain and privation because the Lord gives them the grace to bear it for his sake.

I believe in the power of these still small voices, and I pray that the church of God may never get the idea that she is to depend upon certain great orators and distinguished ministers. I fear that many have fallen into most serious mistakes with regard to this matter; for, when certain great preachers are absent, their places of worship are closed just as if God had gone away to the country or the seaside because Mr So-and-so or Dr So-and-so had gone there.

I pray that you, dear friends, may never put such confidence in any of us as to think that God could not work just as well by other people if he pleased to do so, or to imagine that we must come to you with most elaborately prepared sermons, and always charm your ears with brilliant oratory. As for myself, I abhor all oratory or eloquence except that which comes straight from the heart. The church of Jesus Christ has been greatly injured by the highly polished sermons and speeches of famous orators, but let us, brothers, ever speak in the language that our heart prompts us to use. Let our very soul run over at our lips as it pours itself out, like the gushing stream from an ever-flowing spring, for this is the best kind of eloquence with which we can plead with sinners to forsake their sins, and turn to the living God. Let us be willing to be accounted weak, and to have our speech called contemptible, as Paul's was, for God may then be pleased to bless us as he will not do in any other way.

The point I want to emphasize is this: the reliance of the church, under God, must not be upon the voices that ring out, far and wide, like a peal of bells, nor upon the tongues that give forth the sweet music that pleases the ear. We must rely upon the gospel itself, upon the gospel simply stated, upon the gospel taught in the Sunday school, the gospel explained at the family altar, the gospel lived and loved by holy men and women. It is that which will effectually do the work of God and accomplish his glorious purposes of grace, and I would have all of you who are seeking to serve your Saviour believe that his blessing will rest upon your service even though it may only seem to be as a still small voice.

You, my dear sisters, may not be able to preach a sermon, but you may do what is far better that that. The loving words that you may speak to your children, the helpful hymns that you may teach them as they gather around you, your evening prayer with them as you lay them down to sleep, and your own holy example will all be the still small voice in which God will speak to them. And you who help in caring for the children, and you who teach in the day schools, and you who anywhere are brought into contact with your fellow men, can, by your words and by your actions, bear most important messages for God, even though, in the judgement of mankind, you may be only like a still small voice that seems to have little force in it.

I wish the whole church of Christ would realize that her greatest victories have usually been accomplished by those who did not, from the human standpoint, seem competent for the task, and that she may still expect to see the grandest results coming to her by the use of ordinary means, by ordinary people devoutly exercising, in the name of God, their ordinary functions, in an ordinary way; the workers, however, being under the gracious influence of the divine Spirit from whom all true power must come.

4. A message to sinners

I shall now conclude my discourse by using the text in a fourth way. I believe there was a message to sinners in that still small voice. Now, in the scene which is here sketched by the inspired pen, you have many things that you may well consider. The prophet saw how the great and strong wind tore the mountains and broke the rocks in pieces; he felt the earth reel beneath him and saw the valleys lifted to the hills and the hills sunk into deep glens by the mighty forces of the earthquake; and he saw the forests on the hillsides all ablaze with fire; but God was not revealed to him in any of those terrible sights.

It was only when the still small voice came that God spoke to him, and it is the same in many of those terrors that some seeking souls experience. Human nature is there, the devil is often there, but very frequently God is not there in any saving sense; so none of you should wish to feel those terrors. It is a great mercy when God brings his people to himself by a smoother road than that. I know that some are brought to him by that rough road, and if they are, they may be thankful that they are brought to him anyhow rather than left to perish in their sins. Yet if God, in his great tenderness to others, brings them to himself gently, why should they regret it? Should they not be perfectly satisfied, and even be doubly grateful to be saved without having to endure such trying experiences as many others have had? Beloved friends, do not crave these experiences for yourselves, or else you may in that way provoke God to anger, and he may chasten you in his hot displeasure. You are refusing to do what he bids you do, namely, trust his dear Son, Jesus Christ; and you are wanting him to make you have these horrible feelings, which, if you did have them, you would be only too thankful to lose.

Let me further say to you that, if any of you have felt these dreadful terrors, I implore you not to place any reliance upon them. You will make a fatal mistake if you suppose that you are saved simply because you have been driven almost to despair. There can be no more insecure foundation for a hope of heaven than to think that you are saved because you have realized that you were lost. It would be a very absurd idea for a man to conclude that he was in health because he had felt that he was ill, or for another to imagine that he was rich because he had felt that he was poor.

There is a remorse which is akin to repentance, but it is not the fruit of the grace of God. There is a sense of sin which rises, not from the work of the Spirit of God, but from a man's own conscience, from conscience aroused, yet still unenlightened by God the Holy Spirit. There are few things more terrible than the awakened conscience of a man who still remains unbelieving; yet some have had that dreadful experience, and have even ventured to suppose that they were saved because they had passed through such a period of alarm and horror. If any of you have thus suffered, do not place any reliance upon that experience.

When the still small voice, in which God is, really comes to you, do you know how it will come? Probably in the same way that it came to Elijah. It will address you personally, so that you will begin to feel the personal bearing of the truths to which you have been listening Lord's Day after Lord's Day. As the still small voice said to the prophet, 'What are you doing here, Elijah?', so the truth will begin to question you, and you will then hear every sermon for yourself, and not for other people. When you read the Bible, you will read it for yourself, to find out what it says to you, and through the truth recorded there God will speak to your soul.

But, at first, that still small voice will not comfort you any more than it comforted Elijah. It will put searching questions to you concerning your character and conduct. It will make you look at your past life, and cause you to sorrow over it. It will make you look at your present life, and cause you to blush as you see how sinful it is. It will also make you remember how many years you have wasted in living for yourself and vanity and not living unto God. The still small voice will make you realize at what a distance you are from God, and what a change must be wrought in you before you can be put among his children. It will also make you cast a glance forward to your future life and cause you to tremble at the prospect that lies before you. It will remind you that if you remain unconverted you will go from bad to worse, you will heap up sin upon sin, and your heart will get harder and harder until you are given up to final impenitence.

After this stern message, it will be a blessed thing for you if the still small voice gives you some measure of hope. It may be that there is nothing striking about what you are now feeling. It is no alarming sickness that you have had, it is no wonderful dream that has come to you in your sleep, it is no singular providence that you have experienced; but, somehow or other, wherever you are, you feel ill at ease, you are troubled in spirit and cannot rest. Oh, what a blessed unrest that is which drives a sinner away from his sins! What a sweet bitter thing that is which makes a sinful soul sick of the world, and makes it hunger and thirst after Christ!

I pray the Lord to give this unrest and this hunger and thirst to many of you. I have known some who have had this experience so severely that they could not rest in the workshop; they have done their work, it is true, but it was with many a sigh between. Even their meals seemed to lose the zest they once possessed. When they slept at night their sleep was not restful, and when they woke their sorrow was still upon them. They felt that they could not endure themselves unless they could get right with God. That is the effect of the still small voice when God is in it.

That voice will before long probably change its note in addressing some of you, for it will talk to you about redeeming grace and dying love. It will speak to you about the sinner's Saviour, the Saviour for you, and you will be conscious of a blessed, gentle, persuasive influence inclining you to hear about Jesus, making you attentive to the Word, and moving you to wish to believe in Jesus as your own personal Saviour. And that voice will check you if you begin even to look back towards sin with any desire to return to it, and it will stir up within you more and more holy aspirations till, at last, it will lead you really to look to Jesus and live.

And when you have looked to him, all your life long you will continue to hear that voice; even when others do not hear it, you will. If you attempt to put out your hand to iniquity, you will draw it back with a start because of the warning that voice will utter. Often when others are busy only about the world, your mind will be soaring away to heaven because that voice will be weaning you from the earth and wooing you to be up and away to your Father's house above.

That still small voice will often tell you what to do. 'Your ears shall hear a word behind you, saying, "This is the way, walk in it"' (Isa. 30:21). If you happen to be where you cannot listen to the ministry of the Word, or are not profited by it, that voice will speak to you. As you read the Scriptures, that voice will speak to you with such power as no other voice ever had over your soul; for, after all, it is the voice of Jesus, it is the voice of everlasting love, it is the voice that said upon Calvary, 'It is finished'; it is the voice that said, 'Come to me, all you who labour and are heavy laden, and I will give you rest' (Matt. 11:28); it is the voice that pleads in heaven, 'Father, I desire that they also whom you gave me may be with me where I am, that they may behold my glory' (John 17:24).

Do not, dear friends, be listening for any other voices. Do not expect to have any other revelation beside that which is recorded in this blessed book. You have not only Moses and the prophets, you also have Jesus and the apostles, so hear them. Let the still small voice reveal the truth to you, and do not ask for any other message. This is the all-sufficient guide for you with the illumination of the Holy Spirit, so do not seek for any other. If you have been saved by it, I charge you to obey it in every jot and tittle. Do not alter any ordinance of God, and do not forget any of his precepts, but follow the Lamb wherever he goes. Wherever you see the print of his pierced foot, there put down your own foot. Do as he did, be as he was; and then soon you will be where he is. May his blessed Spirit and his still small voice be with you till you see his face without a veil between, for his dear name's sake! Amen.

The Word and the Spirit

Chapter 5

The sealing of the Spirit

The word of the Lord is the sole foundation upon which faith builds. Some people have a sort of confidence in God, but they are also looking out for confirming signs, and they spoil the simplicity of their faith by having one eye on Christ and another eye on their peace of mind.

5.
The sealing of the Spirit

In him you also trusted, after you heard the word of truth, the gospel of your salvation; in whom also, having believed, you were sealed with the Holy Spirit of promise, who is the guarantee of our inheritance until the redemption of the purchased possession, to the praise of his glory —
Eph. 1:13-14

A sermon delivered on Lord's Day morning, 19 March 1876, by C. H. Spurgeon.
Sermon No. 1284

I have taken the whole passage for the sake of completing the sense, but I have no intention whatever of preaching upon all of it. Practically I only need for this topic the following words: 'Also, having believed, you were sealed with the Holy Spirit of promise.' The sealing of the Holy Spirit will be the subject of our meditation. There are many who have believed in the Lord Jesus Christ who are extremely anxious to obtain some token for good, some witness from God which shall render them quite sure that they are saved. They have not yet reached the full assurance of faith, and they feel uneasy till they attain it. They feel that these matters are too important to be left at all uncertain, and they, therefore, pine for some sure witness or seal. Men will not risk their estates, and no spiritually sensible man will endure to have his soul and its eternal affairs in jeopardy for an hour: hence this anxiety. It is true that by the way of faith only the fullest and best assurance may be reached, but many who do truly believe in the Lord Jesus Christ are not yet aware of this, and their trembling hearts crave for a testimonial from the infallible God to certify them that they are indeed saved. Yes, and I conceive that even more advanced saints, who know more fully where their standing is, and confess that they can only walk by faith, yet often sing with very great emphasis of desire —

> Might I but hear thy heavenly tongue
> But whisper 'Thou art mine,'
> That cheerful word should raise my song
> To notes almost divine.

Though we can and do believe, and can claim the privilege which belongs to those who have not seen and yet have believed, yet we would be glad to have a sight sometimes. We sometimes wish we could know by sure mark and evidence and token that our experience is after all a reality, and that we are indeed born of God.

> O tell me that my worthless name
> Is graven on thy hands!
> Show me some promise in thy book
> Where my salvation stands!

Now, in the best sense, this seal which we seek after is to be had; more than that, it is manifestly seen by many of God's children. It does not supersede faith, but it rewards and strengthens it. There is a way by which God does speak to his own and assure them that they are his; there is a pledge and an earnest, and this is freely given to the people of God. May God's own Spirit enable me to speak correctly upon this weighty subject.

The text says, 'Having believed, you were sealed with the Holy Spirit of promise'; and, therefore, first, I shall call your attention to the position of this sealing; secondly, to the benefits which arise out of it; and thirdly, to the sealing itself, which, indeed, I shall endeavour to explain all through.

1. The position of the sealing with the Spirit

First, let us speak of the position of this sealing. We desire some confirming seal from God set upon our souls, some sure token that we are indeed his own people. That sealing we can have, God does bestow it; but let us notice very carefully, lest we make a mistake, where that sealing comes in.

Not before believing

It does not come before believing. According to the text it is 'Having believed, you were sealed.' Now, there are hundreds of people who are craving something to see or to feel before they will believe in Jesus Christ; this is wickedness and the result of an unbelief which is most offensive in the sight of God.

If you demand a token before you believe, you practically say that you cannot take God's bare word for your comfort, that the sure word of testimony recorded in the Bible is not enough for you, that the solemn declaration of God may after all be false; at any rate, that you find it impossible to repose your confidence upon that alone, and must see something beside. If not a miracle, perhaps you demand a dream, or a strange feeling, or a mysterious operation; at any rate, if you do not see some sign and wonder, you declare that you will not believe. You do, in fact, say to God, 'If you will not go out of your way to give me what I ask, and to do for me what I demand, then I will call you a liar to your face, by refusing to believe on you.' Ah, this will not do; this is to provoke the Lord to jealousy, and he that does this will receive no token whatsoever, unless it is the sign of the unbelievers of Chorazin, for whom the day of judgement shall be more intolerable than for Sodom and Gomorrah.

Not necessarily at the same instant as faith

Note also that this sealing does not necessarily come at once with faith. It grows out of faith, and comes 'after that you believed' (AV). We are not in every case sealed at the moment when we first trust in Jesus. I am persuaded that many who believe in Jesus enter into peace directly, and perceive at once the blessed assurance which is involved in their possessing the Holy Spirit; but with many others it is not so.

I have frequently been asked this question, 'What is a person to do who does believe in Jesus, but yet is not conscious of peace and joy, but is filled with such a conflict within that the utmost he can do is to cling to Jesus with trembling hope?' I have replied, 'If you believe in Jesus Christ you are saved; the best evidence that you are saved lies in the assurance of the Word of God that every believer has eternal hope.'

Whether you feel that you are justified or not is not the point. You are to accept God's Word, which assures you that everyone who believes is justified. You are bound to believe the testimony of God apart from the supporting evidence of inward experience, and if it were possible for you to be a believer by the year together, and yet to find no peace, still you would have no right to doubt what God says because you do not feel peace; you are bound to hold on to God's promise whether you enjoy peace or not.

My firm belief is that where there is a real faith in the promise of God, peace and the other fruits of the Spirit come as a necessary ultimate consequence, but even then they are not grounds of faith. The word of the Lord is the sole foundation upon which faith builds. Some people have a sort of confidence in God, but they are also looking out for confirming signs, and they spoil the simplicity of their faith by having one eye on Christ and another eye on their peace of mind. Now, my friend, this will never do. You are bound to believe in God as he is revealed in Christ Jesus unto salvation, altogether apart from peace, joy, or anything else. The witness of the Spirit within is not the ground nor the cause of our faith. Faith comes by hearing, and hearing by the word of God.

I, being a sinner, believe that Jesus Christ came into the world to save sinners, and I rest my soul upon him, believing that he will save me; this is to be my standing, seal or no seal, token or no token. My dependence is not to be upon the seal of the Spirit, but upon the blood of the Son. The Spirit of God never takes the place of the Redeemer. He exercises his own peculiar office, which is to take the things of Christ and show them to us, and not to put his own things in the place of Jesus. The foundation of our hope is laid in Christ from first to last, and if we rest there we are saved.

The seal does not always come with faith, but it follows after. I have said this because I am afraid lest in any way whatever you should leave the simple, plain, and solid ground of confidence in the finished work of Jesus Christ, and in that only. Recollect that a man who believes in Jesus Christ is as truly saved when he does not know it as he is when he does know it; he is as truly the Lord's when he mourns in the valley of humiliation as when he sings on the mountain top of joy and fellowship.

Our ground of trust is not to be found in our experience, but in the person and work of our Lord Jesus.

> I dare not trust the sweetest frame;
> But wholly lean on Jesus' name:
> On Christ the solid rock I stand,
> All other ground is sinking sand.

Not the final thing in the Christian life

Note, also, as to the position of this sealing, that, while it is not the first, it also is not the last thing in the divine life. It comes after believing, but when you obtain it there is something yet to follow.

Perhaps you have had the notion that if you could once be told from the mouth of God himself that you were saved, you would then lie down and cease from life's struggle. It is clear, therefore, that such an assurance should be an evil thing for you, for a Christian is never more out of place than when he dreams that he has ceased from conflict. The natural, fit, and proper position for a soldier of Jesus Christ is to be at war with sin. We are wrestlers, and our normal condition is that of 'striving according to his working which works in me mightily' (Col. 1:29).

This side of heaven, if there is a place for nest-building and ease-taking, it is not the place for you. You are a pilgrim, and a pilgrim's business is to be on the road, pressing forward to the home beyond. Remember, if there are seats of ease — and no doubt there are — they are not for you, since you are a runner in a great race, with heaven and earth for witnesses. Cessation from watchfulness means ruin to your soul; the closing of conflict would show that you could never gain the victory, and perfect rest on earth would show that none remained for you in heaven.

Even if the Spirit of God should seal you, what will it amount to? To the inheritance itself, so that you can say, 'I have attained perfection'? Certainly not. No, brothers, the Scripture says, 'Who is the guarantee of our inheritance until the redemption of the purchased possession.'

All these things that you cannot obtain this side of heaven are a promise of the perfection of which heaven is made up:

> There rest shall follow toil,
> And ease succeed to care:
> The victors there divide the spoil;
> They sing and triumph there.

Here we must labour, watch, run, fight, wrestle, agonize; all our forces, strengthened by the eternal Spirit, must be expended in this high enterprise, striving to enter in at the narrow gate. When we have obtained the sealing our warfare is not ended; we have only then received a foretaste of the victory, for which we must still fight on. This is the true position of the sealing: it stands between the grace which enables us to believe and the glory which is our promised inheritance.

2. The benefits of the sealing with the Spirit

We will notice, secondly, what the benefits are of this sealing, and while we are doing so, we shall be compelled to state what we think that sealing is, though that is to be the subject of the third head.

The sealing in relation to God's promises

The sealing spoken of in the text does not make the promises of God to be true. Please notice that. This text has been preached upon as though it stated that the Spirit of God set his seal upon the gospel and the promises of God. Well, dear friends, it is true that the Spirit of God witnesses to the truth and to the sureness of the promises, but that is evidently not intended here, for the text does not say that the promises were sealed, but that 'You were sealed.' You are the writing which has the stamp put upon it; you yourselves are sealed.

It is not even stated that the Spirit of God seals up covenant blessings as gold is sealed up in a bag, and reserves them for the chosen people of God; the text tells us that believers themselves are thus reserved and marked as the Lord's peculiar treasure, and it is upon believers themselves that this seal of the Holy Spirit is set.

No, brothers, the Holy Spirit does not make the promises sure, they are sure of themselves; God who cannot lie has uttered them, and therefore they cannot fail. Nor, my brothers, does the Holy Spirit make sure our interest in those promises; that interest in the promises was sure in the divine decree, before the earth was, and is a matter of fact which cannot be changed. The promises are already sure to all the chosen people of God. The Holy Spirit makes us sure that the word is true and that we are concerned in it, but the promise was sure beforehand, and our interest in that promise was sure, too, from the moment in which it was bestowed upon us by the sovereign act of God.

The sealing in relation to Christ

To understand our text, you must notice that it is bounded by two words, 'in whom' (AV); these two words are given twice in this verse: 'In whom after that you believed, you were sealed.' What is meant by 'in whom'? The words signify 'in Christ'. It is in Christ that the people of God are sealed. We must therefore understand this sealing as it would relate to Christ, since so far, and so far only, can it relate to us. Was our Lord sealed? Turn to John 6:27, and there you have this exhortation: 'Do not labour for the food which perishes, but for the food which endures to everlasting life, which the Son of Man will give you, because God the Father has set his seal on him.' There is the clue to our text. 'God the Father has set his seal on him'; since our sealing is in him, it must be the same sealing.

Notice, then, first, that the ever-blessed Son was sealed on the Father's part by God's giving a testimony to him that he was indeed his own Son, and the sent one of the Lord. As when a king issues a proclamation, he sets his seal manual to it to say, 'This is mine'; so when the Father sent his Son into the world, he gave him this testimony: 'This is my beloved Son, in whom I am well pleased' (Matt. 3:17). He said this in words, but how did he give a perpetual testimony by a seal which should be with him throughout life? It was by anointing him with the Holy Spirit. The seal that Jesus was the Messiah was that the Spirit of God rested upon him without measure. Hence we read expressions like these: 'He was justified in the Spirit' (1 Tim. 3:16). 'He was declared to be the Son of God with power, according to the Spirit of holiness, by the resurrection from the dead' (Rom. 1:4). 'It is the Spirit who bears witness, because the Spirit is truth' (1 John 5:6).

Now, the Spirit of God, wherever it abides upon a man, is the mark that that man is accepted of God. We do not say that where the Spirit merely strives at intervals there is any seal of divine favour, but where he abides it is assuredly so. The very fact that we possess the Spirit of God is God's testimony and seal in us that we are his, and that as he has sent his Son into the world, even so he sends us into the world.

Secondly, to our Lord Jesus Christ the Holy Spirit was a seal for his own encouragement. Our Lord condescended to restrain the power of his own Godhead, and as a servant he depended upon the Father for support. When he began his ministry he encouraged himself thus: 'The Spirit of the Lord is upon me, because ... he has sent me to heal the broken-hearted' (Isa. 61:1; Luke 4:18). He found his stimulus of service, he found the authorization of his service, he found his comfort and strength for service, in the fact that God had given him the Holy Spirit. This was his joy.

Now, brothers and sisters, if we want to be encouraged for holy service by feeling quite sure that we are saved, from where must we get that encouragement? Read 1 John 3:24, where the seal of God is described: 'And by this we know that he abides in us, by the Spirit whom he has given us.' Read also in the fourth chapter, verse 13, 'By this we know that we abide in him, and he in us, because he has given us of his Spirit.' The seal that comforted our Lord, and that made him to know in times of depression that he was indeed beloved of the Father, was that he had the Spirit of God. In the same way, brethren, to you and to me, the possession of the Spirit of God is our continuous encouragement, for by this we may know beyond all question that we dwell in God and God dwells in us. The seal answers a two-fold purpose; it is on God's part a testimony, and to us an encouragement.

But thirdly, the seal is meant to be a piece of evidence to others. The Father set his seal upon his Son in order that others might discern that he was indeed sent of God. John says, 'I did not know him, but he who sent me to baptize with water said to me, "Upon whom you see the Spirit descending, and remaining on him, this is he who baptizes with the Holy Spirit." And I have seen and testified that this is the Son of God' (John 1:33-34).

The Spirit, then, was upon our Lord the seal for recognition, and, beloved, so must it be with us. We cannot be known by our fellow Christians except by the possession of the Spirit of God. Have you ever noticed how Peter claimed for the uncircumcised the rights of church membership in Acts 15:8-9? He says, 'God, who knows the heart, acknowledged them, by giving them the Holy Spirit just as he did to us, and made no distinction between us and them, purifying their hearts by faith.'

To Peter, the possession of the Holy Spirit was the broad seal of heaven which the Lord never sets upon a heart wherein there is no faith. The same argument had been felt in all its power by him when he said, 'Can anyone forbid water, that these should not be baptized who have received the Holy Spirit just as we have?' (Acts 10:47).

Paul used this as his test concerning the sons of men; for in Romans 8:9, he says, 'You are not in the flesh, but in the Spirit, if indeed the Spirit of God dwells in you. Now if anyone does not have the Spirit of Christ, he is not his,' plainly indicating that the absence of the Spirit is fatal, for the divine signature is not at the bottom of the document. But if the Spirit of God is there, then all is right, for the Lord never puts his seal to anything which is not sound and true. Rest quite sure that where the Spirit of God abides, there the gospel of Jesus Christ has been written on the heart, and the man is saved.

Further, the fourth effect of the seal upon Christ was that it was to the world a witness. The Spirit of God upon Jesus Christ was not recognized by the ungodly world to be indeed divine, but they perceived and were astonished at something about him that they did not understand. He spoke with authority and not as the scribes, and they confessed, 'No man ever spoke like this man!' (John 7:46). They did not know what spirit he was of, but they knew they hated it, and immediately they began to oppose him.

Now, brothers and sisters, if you have the same seal as your Lord, which is described in the text as 'the Spirit of promise', the same result will follow: men will wonder at you, misunderstand you, and oppose you. And what is the reason? Never in this world did the Spirit of promise appear without opposition from the spirit of bondage. Isaac was the child of promise, and did not Ishmael, who was born after the flesh, persecute him? The two seeds, of the flesh and of the promise, are at daggers drawn with each other. When the Lord sets his seal upon you by giving you the Spirit of promise, so that you are not under the law but under Christ, the world will know it; they will not admire you; they will strive against you to destroy you.

Once more, the seal upon our Lord Jesus Christ was intended for a fifth reason, namely, for his perseverance even to the end. A seal is set upon a treasure which we mean to preserve; and so was the precious Redeemer sealed. Now, you will say to me,

'But dare we speak of Jesus Christ as being preserved by the Spirit of God?' My dear brothers, we must never forget the wonderful self-denial of Christ in that he laid aside his own divine power, and while he was in this world he said the Father was greater than he, and he became a man so as to pray, and to believe, and to depend upon the Father.

Jesus Christ put himself into such a condition while he was here that he relied upon the Spirit of God to uphold him. Do you doubt it? Turn to Isaiah 42, and you there get it in express words: 'Behold my Servant whom I uphold!' See how he puts himself, as a servant, to be upheld by the Lord: 'My Elect One in whom my soul delights! I have put my Spirit upon him; he will bring forth justice to the Gentiles. He will not cry out, nor raise his voice, nor cause his voice to be heard in the street. A bruised reed he will not break, and smoking flax he will not quench; he will bring forth justice for truth' (Isa. 42:1-3). There can be no doubt that this is Christ; for these very words are quoted concerning himself.

Now, what comes of the upholding of the blessed Spirit? 'He will not fail nor be discouraged till he has established justice in the earth, and the coastlands shall wait for his law' (Isa. 42:4). So the Spirit of God upheld Christ and sustained him and kept him till his life's work was finished, without his failing or being discouraged. My brothers, this is how you and I must be kept; this is the seal which we need, which will preserve us as the consecrated ones of God, so that when he comes, he will find us under seal and safe.

Let me now recapitulate. Upon our Lord Jesus the Spirit of God acted as a seal, namely, as God's testimony that he was his Son, as an encouragement to his own heart, as evidence to others, as a witness to the world, and as a help to perseverance, even to the end. The sealing of the Spirit will confer the same benefits upon us: 'In whom also, having believed, you were sealed with the Holy Spirit of promise.'

3. Marks of the sealing with the Spirit

Thirdly, let us consider the sealing itself. A great deal has been said on this point which has tended to foster superstition. Some have supposed that there is a separate act of the Spirit of God in which he seals believers. It may be so — I will not raise the question; but I should be very sorry if any man here, living in sin, should nevertheless look back upon some time of religious excitement or enjoyment and say, 'I am safe, for on that occasion I was sealed'; and I should be very sorry to have any brother take as the sure reason why he is saved some remarkable experience which he underwent on a certain day long past. A seal is for the present, and is not a mere memory, but an object palpable now, and before the eyes. I am afraid many have been deceived into carelessness by the notion of a sealing received long ago.

Let us seek out the truth. According to the text, as far as I can read it, here is a man who has believed in Jesus, and he desires a seal that God loves him. God gives him the Spirit, and that is all the seal he can wish for or expect. Nothing more is wanted, nothing else would be so good. The very fact that the Spirit of God works in you to will and to do, according to God's good pleasure, is your seal; you do not require anything beyond. I do not say that any one operation of the Holy Spirit is to be regarded as the seal; but the whole of them together, as they prove his being within us, make up that seal.

It is better, however, to keep to the doctrine that the Spirit of God in the believer is himself the seal:

Thou art the earnest of his love,
The pledge of joys to come,
And thy soft wings, celestial dove,
Will safe convey me home.

Wisdom and revelation

Now, let us look at what the context tells us about this. If you read on, the apostle tells us that *wisdom* and *revelation* in the knowledge of God are part of the seal. Kindly turn to the chapter and follow out the apostle's line of argument. He says, 'Therefore I also, after I heard of your faith in the Lord Jesus and your love for all the saints, do not cease to give thanks for you, making mention of you in my prayers; that the God of our Lord Jesus Christ, the Father of glory, may give to you the spirit of wisdom and revelation in the knowledge of him' (vv. 15-17).

See, then, if you have believed in Jesus Christ, the Spirit of God comes upon you, and he gives you wisdom and revelation. Doctrines in the Word which you never understood before become clear to you — 'the eyes of your understanding being enlightened' (v. 18); the blessings promised are more distinctly discerned, and you see 'the hope of his calling, what are the riches of the glory of his inheritance in the saints' (v. 18). The deeper truths, which at first quite staggered and puzzled you, gradually open up to you, and you see and appreciate them.

More especially you discover the glory of Christ and see the exceeding greatness of the power with which the Lord works in the saints, 'according to the working of his power, which he worked in Christ when he raised him from the dead, and seated him at his right hand in the heavenly places, far above all principality and power and might and dominion, and every name that is named, not only in this age but also in that which is to come' (vv. 19-21). You drink deep into the blessed thought that Jesus is 'to be head over all things to the church' (v. 22), and you obtain some glimpses into the mysterious doctrine that the church is his fullness, 'the fullness of him who fills all in all' (v. 23).

Now, brothers, if we know correctly these things the Spirit has taught us, and the consequence of it is that we say to ourselves, 'Certainly I must be a child of God, for I never understood the things of God before. How could I have learned them if I had not been taught of God?' The Master seems to stand by our side and say, 'Blessed are you, Simon Bar-Jonah: for flesh and blood has not revealed this to you, but my Father who is in heaven' (Matt. 16:17).

If you have been made to see the abounding grace of God, the grandeur of the plan of salvation, and the choice beauties of the blessed person of Jesus Christ, you have a sure seal upon your soul, for like the blind man in the gospels you can say, 'One thing I know: that though I was blind, now I see' (John 9:25).

Life

Following on to the next chapter you will see that the Spirit of God works *life* in every man who possesses him, and that life becomes another form of the seal: 'You he made alive, who were dead in trespasses and sins' (Eph. 2:1). That life is of a new kind, and has a renewing power, so that men forsake the course of this world, and no longer fulfil the desires of the flesh and of the mind. This new life they trace to God, who is rich in mercy, who in his great love with which he loved them, even when they were dead in sins, has made them alive together with Christ. They trace this life entirely to the grace of God — 'By grace you have been saved' (Eph. 2:8); and they see that this life produces in them good works, 'For we are his workmanship, created in Christ Jesus for good works' (Eph. 2:10).

I do not need to explain how this life lifts us up to sit in the heavenlies with Christ, for most of you know all about it. You have received a life from above, a living and incorruptible seed is in you, you have passed into a new world, you have feelings, desires, fears, hopes, such as you never knew before, and thus your outward life is also changed, so that you follow after that which is according to the will of God.

Now, brothers, what can be a better seal to you that you are indeed saved than this life which you feel within? This is the way in which the Spirit of God seals you, by making you partakers of the divine life, which never yet did reside in the unbeliever, and never can dwell apart from faith. To 'As many as received him, to them he gave the right to become children of God, even to those who believe in his name' (John 1:12). 'He who believes in the Son has everlasting life; and he who does not believe the Son shall not see life, but the wrath of God abides on him' (John 3:36). So that wisdom and life, which are both sure results of the indwelling of the Spirit of God, are a seal to us that we are really saved.

Fellowship with other believers

Go on a little further and you will notice upon the one seal a further mark, namely, *fellowship*: 'You were without Christ, being aliens from the commonwealth of Israel, and strangers from the covenants of promise, having no hope and without God in the world. But now in Christ Jesus you who once were far off are have been made near by the blood of Christ. For he himself is our peace, who has made both one, and has broken down the middle wall of division between us' (Eph. 2:12-14).

Those who have believed in Jesus Christ are led by the Spirit of God to love their fellow Christians, and in this way 'We know that we have passed from death to life, because we love the brethren' (1 John 3:14). Once we thought the godly a dull and melancholy set — at any rate we let them go their own way — and we were glad to keep aloof from them; but now we delight in their society, sympathize with their pursuits, and are willing to share their persecutions. We count the saints of God the best company in the world; we would sooner sit down and talk half an hour with a poor, bedridden Christian woman, than be found in the courts of princes. This brotherly love becomes a seal of grace within our hearts, for John tells us in his first epistle,

'Everyone who loves is born of God and knows God. If we love one another, God abides in us, and his love has been perfected in us' (1 John 4:7,12).

Fellowship with God

Even more striking is that which follows, namely, that we have *fellowship with God*. The apostle speaks of us as being reconciled unto God by the cross, by which the enmity is slain, and he says of our Lord, 'For through him we both have access by one Spirit to the Father' (Eph. 2:18). I am following the course of the chapter. When you and I feel that we commune with God, that there is no quarrel between him and us, that he is loved by us as we are loved by him, that we can draw near to him in prayer and speak to him, that he hears us and deigns to grant us gracious answers of peace — these are blessed seals of salvation. Some of us can look back on times of fellowship with God, on seasons of prevailing prayer with him, and upon countless answers to our petitions: all these become to us infallible tokens of divine love.

Growth

I shall not tire you if I bid you notice that the apostle next speaks of being built up: 'Having been built on the foundation of the apostles and prophets, Jesus Christ himself being the chief cornerstone, in whom the whole building, being joined together, grows into a holy temple in the Lord' (Eph. 2:20-21). Are you not conscious, believers, that you are being built up unto a divinely glorious form, after a high and noble model? It does not yet appear what we shall be, but you must be conscious that course upon course of precious stones have been built upon the foundation of your faith in Christ. Since you have known the Lord you have made a distinct advance. At times you are afraid you have only grown downwards, but you have grown; there is a something about you now which was not there ten years ago.

I am distinctly conscious, somehow, that twenty years ago I was not what I now am. I sometimes feel like a bird in the eggshell! I am chipping it away bit by bit, I believe it will break one of these days, and the bird will come out; but I often feel my wings fretted and cramped by the shell; I want the life in me to be developed and set free. Do you never feel the same? Have you not felt as if you yourself were big with a far more glorious nature, and longed for deliverance from flesh and frailty? These groanings, aspirations, hopes, and desires are all seals of salvation; you will never find the ungodly moved in this way. These pangs are peculiar to life.

You are not a finished structure, but a house in process of erection, and you may be sure that one of these days the capstone will be brought forth with shouts of 'Grace, grace to it' (Zech. 4:7). But this upbuilding through the Spirit of God is the seal of the Spirit; it is to you the evidence that God has begun a good work in you, and is carrying it on.

Indwelling of the Spirit

Last of all, the second chapter finishes up by saying, 'In whom you also are being built together for a habitation of God in the Spirit'; and this seems to me to gather up all that I have said before. The *indwelling of the Spirit* in the saints, in the whole of them united, and in each one in particular, is a choice seal:

> Dost thou not dwell in all the saints,
> And seal them heirs of heaven?

Yes, that is the manner of the sealing, according to the prayer of our hymn —

> Jesus, my Lord, reveal

In charms of grace divine,
And be thyself the sacred seal,
That pearl of price is mine.

If you have the Spirit of God dwelling in you, you must be the Lord's. Will the Spirit of God dwell in any temple but that which God has consecrated? He may come upon men to strive with them for a while, but he will never dwell in any heart that has not been cleansed with the blood of Jesus. Nor can he possibly reside permanently in any soul which is defiled with self-righteousness and love of sin. No, beloved, if the Spirit of God dwells in you, you need no dreams, nor angels' whispers, nor noises in the air. The indwelling Spirit is the only seal you need. I put the question to you, brothers and sisters: what more do you want? What more could God give you?

Suppose you were to meet on the road home, standing on the snow, an angel, clothed in glittering white, and that he should say to you, 'I have a message from God to you' — should then mention your name and add, 'You are one of God's chosen.' That vision would comfort you for half an hour, I have no doubt; but many desponding spirits would not be comforted much longer, for the devil would say, 'It was snowing? No doubt the flakes blew into your eyes; or else you have a fine imagination.' 'Oh,' you would say, 'but I heard him speak.' Ah, you had noises in your head; you are becoming a fair subject for Bedlam. I confess if you were to tell me the story, I should not make any bones about it, but should say, 'You are not such a fool as to believe that, are you?' and you would find many other people of the same mind.

Now there can be no doubt about the seal of the text. You have been taught by God what no one but the Spirit of God could have taught you; you have a life in you which no one but the Spirit could have given you: of that knowledge and that life you are perfectly conscious; you do not want to ask anybody else about them. A man may ask me whether I know so and so;

but I am the best witness whether I do or not. I may be asked, 'How do you know you are alive?' Well, I walk about, that is all; but I am quite sure about it, and I do not want any further evidence.

The best seal to a man's heart must be that of which he is conscious, and about which he needs not appeal to others. Give me a seal that is as sure as my own existence: I fail to see how God himself can give me anything more sure than the gift of his Spirit working knowledge and life in me. 'Oh,' says one, 'if only I could hear a voice.' Suppose you did. Then the argument of fear would be that there are countless voices, and one may be mistaken for another. You were in the street when you heard it; perhaps it was a parrot or a starling in the upper window. Who knows? It is so easy for the ear to be deceived. Many a time you have said, 'I know I heard so and so,' when you did not hear it, but something very like it. I would not believe my own ears, if their evidence had to do with my soul, one half so readily as I would believe my own consciousness. Since knowledge and life and other things I have mentioned just now are all matters of consciousness, they are much better seals than anything could be which appealed like an angelic vision to the eye, or like a mysterious voice to the ear. Here you have something sure and steadfast. If the Spirit of God dwells in you, you are his, and if he does not dwell in you, you are not one of his.

Take this for the closing word: 'Do not grieve the Holy Spirit of God, by whom you were sealed for the day of redemption', but love him, honour him, and obey him; so the seal will always be bright before your eyes. As to you who have not believed, I conclude with this sentence: Do not ask for seals; you have nothing to do with seals, but with Jesus. 'An evil and adulterous generation seeks after a sign' (Matt. 12:39). Believe in Christ Jesus, and when you have trusted him, then there will come signs, seals, marks. God bless you, for Christ's sake. Amen.

The Word and the Spirit

Chapter 6

The sword of the Spirit

One might have thought, from what we have seen recently, that orders had come from headquarters that the soldiers were to lay down the sword of the Spirit, the Word of God, and take to lighter weapons.

6.
The sword of the Spirit

Take the sword of the Spirit, which is the word of God —
Eph. 6:17

A sermon delivered on Lord's Day morning, 19 April 1891, by
C. H. Spurgeon.
Sermon No. 2201

To be a Christian is to be a warrior. The good soldier of Jesus Christ must not expect to find ease in this world; it is a battlefield. Neither must he reckon upon the friendship of the world; for that would be enmity against God. His occupation is war. As he puts on piece by piece of the full armour provided for him, he may wisely say to himself, 'This warns me of danger; this prepares me for warfare; this prophesies opposition.'

Difficulties meet us even in standing our ground; for the apostle two or three times bids us, 'Stand.' In the rush of the fight, men are apt to be carried off their legs. If they can keep their footing they will be victorious, but if they are borne down by the rush of their adversaries everything is lost. You are to put on the heavenly armour in order that you may stand, and you will need it to maintain the position in which your captain has placed you. If even to stand requires all this care, judge what the warfare must be! The apostle also speaks of withstanding as well as standing. We are not merely to defend, but also to assail. It is not enough that you are not conquered; you have to conquer; and so we find that we are to take, not only a helmet to protect the head, but also a sword with which to annoy the foe. Ours, therefore, is a stern conflict, standing and withstanding; and we shall want all the armour from the divine magazine, all the strength from the mighty God of Jacob.

It is clear from our text that our defence and our conquest must be obtained by sheer fighting. Many try compromise, but if you are a true Christian, you can never do this business well. The language of deceit does not fit a holy tongue. The adversary is the father of lies, and those that are with him understand the art of equivocation, but saints abhor it. If we discuss terms of peace, and attempt to gain something by policy, we have entered upon a course from which we shall return in disgrace. We have no order from our captain to patch up a truce and get as good terms as we can. We are not sent out to offer concessions. It is said that if we yield a little, perhaps the world will yield a little also, and good may come of it. If we are not too strict and narrow, perhaps sin will kindly consent to be more decent. Our association with it will prevent its being so barefaced and atrocious. If we are not narrow-minded, our broad doctrine will go down well with the world, and they will not be so keen to embrace false teachings as they now are. No such thing. Assuredly this is not the order which our captain has issued. When peace is to be made, he will make it himself, or he will tell us how to behave to that end; but at present our orders are very different.

Neither may we hope to gain by being neutral or granting an occasional truce. We are not to cease from conflict, and try to be as agreeable as we can with our Lord's foes, frequenting their assemblies, and tasting their dainties. No such orders are written here. You are to grasp your weapon and go forth to fight.

Neither may you so much as dream of winning the battle by accident. No man was ever holy by a happy chance. Infinite damage may be done by carelessness, but no man ever won life's battle by it. To let things go on as they please is to let them bear us down to hell. We have no orders to be quiet, and take matters easily. No; we are to pray always, and watch constantly. The one note that rings out from the text is this: 'Take the sword! Take the sword!' No longer is it, talk and debate! No longer is it, parley and compromise! The word of thunder is 'Take the sword.' The captain's voice is clear as a trumpet — 'Take the sword!' No Christian here will have been obedient to our text unless with clear, sharp, and decisive firmness, courage, and resolve, he takes the sword. We must go to heaven sword in hand, all the way. 'Take the sword.' On this command I would enlarge. May the Holy Spirit help me!

It is noteworthy that there is only one weapon of offence provided, although there are several pieces of armour. The Roman soldier usually carried a spear as well as a sword. We have seen frequent representations of the legionary standing upon guard as sentry, and he almost always stands with a spear in his right hand, while his sword hangs at his side. But Paul, for excellent reasons, concentrates our offensive weapon in one, because it answers for all. We are to use the sword, and only the sword. Therefore, if you are going to this fight, see well to your only weapon. If you are to have no other, take care that you have this always in your hand. Let the captain's voice ring in your ear, 'Take the sword! Take the sword!', and so go forth to the field.

Notice, first, the sword you are to take is the sword of the Spirit, which is the Word of God. That is our first point; and the second is equally upon the surface of the text: This sword is to be ours. We are ordered to take the sword of the Spirit, and so make it our own sword.

1. The sword of the Spirit described

First, the Word of God which is to be our one weapon is of noble origin; for it is the sword of the Spirit. It has the properties of a sword, and those were given it by the Spirit of God. Here we note that the Holy Spirit has a sword. He is quiet as the dew, tender as the anointing oil, soft as the zephyr of eventide, and peaceful as a dove; and yet, under another aspect, he wields a deadly weapon. He is the Spirit of judgement and the Spirit of burning, and he does not bear the sword in vain. Of him it may be said, 'The Lord is a man of war: Jehovah is his name' (Ex. 15:3).

The Word of God in the hand of the Spirit wounds very terribly, and makes the heart of man to bleed. Do you not remember, some of you, when you used to be gashed with this sword Sunday after Sunday? Were you not cut to the heart by it, so as to be angry with it? You almost made up your mind to turn away from hearing the gospel again. That sword pursued you, and pierced you in the secrets of your soul, and made you bleed in a thousand places. At last you were 'pricked in the heart', which is a far better thing than being 'cut to the heart'; and then execution was done indeed. That wound was deadly, and none but he that killed could make you alive. Do you recollect how, after this, your sins were slain one after another? Their necks were laid on the block, and the Spirit acted as an executioner with his sword. After that, blessed be God, your fears and doubts and despair and unbelief were also hacked to pieces by this same sword. The Word gave you life; but it was at the first a great killer. Your soul was like a battlefield after a great fight, under the first operations of the divine Spirit, whose sword did not return empty from the conflict.

Beloved, the Spirit of God has war with the Amalek of evil and error from generation to generation. He will spare none of the evils which now pollute the nations; his sword will never be quiet till all these Canaanites are destroyed. The Holy Spirit glorifies Christ not only by what he reveals but also by what he overturns. The strife may be weary, but it will be carried on from age to age, till the Lord Jesus appears; for the Spirit of God will ever espouse the cause of love against hate, of truth against error, of holiness against sin, of Christ against Satan. He will win the day, and those who are with him will in his might be more than conquerors. The Holy Spirit has proclaimed war and wields a two-edged sword.

The Holy Spirit wields no sword but the Word of God. This wonderful book, which contains the utterances of God's mouth, is the one weapon which the Holy Spirit elects to use for his warlike purposes. It is a spiritual weapon, and so is suitable to the Holy Spirit. The weapons of his warfare are not carnal; he never uses either persecution or patronage, force or bribery, glitter of grandeur or terror of power. He works upon men by the Word, which is suitable to his own spiritual nature, and to the spiritual work which is to be accomplished.

While it is spiritual, this weapon is 'mighty through God'. So sharp is this sword that a cut from the Word of God will cleave a man's spirit from head to foot. Though by long practice in sin a man may have coated himself as with impenetrable mail, yet the Word of the Lord will divide the northern iron and the steel. The Holy Spirit can make a man feel the divine power of the sacred Word in the very centre of his being. For battling with the spirits of man, or with spirits of an infernal kind, there is no weapon so keen, so piercing, so able to divide between the joints and marrow, so penetrating as to the thoughts and intents of the heart. The Word, in the Spirit's hand, gives no dash-wound, but cuts into the man's heart, and so wounds him that there is no healing except by supernatural power. The wounded conscience will bleed; its pains will be upon it day and night; and though it seek out a thousand medicines, no salve but one can cure a gash which this terrible sword has made.

This weapon is two-edged; indeed, it is all edge, and whichever way it strikes, it wounds and kills. There is no such a thing as the flat of the sword of the Spirit; it has a razor edge every way. Beware how you handle it, you critics; it may wound even you. It will cut you to your destruction, one of these days, unless you are converted. He that uses the Word in the Lord's battles may use it upon carnal hopes, and then strike back upon unbelieving fears; he may smite with one edge the love of sin, and then with the other the pride of self-righteousness. It is a conquering weapon in all ways, this wondrous sword of the Spirit of God.

The Word, we say, is the only sword which the Spirit uses. I know the Holy Spirit uses gracious sermons, but it is only in proportion as they have the Word of God in them. I know the Holy Spirit uses religious books, but only so far as they are the Word of God told out in other language. Conviction, conversion, and consolation still are produced only by the Word of God.

Learn, then, the wisdom of using the Word of God for holy purposes. The Spirit has abundant ability to speak of his own self, apart from the written Word. The Holy Spirit is God, and therefore he is the greatest spirit in the universe. All wisdom dwells in him. He thought out the laws which govern nature and direct providence.

The Holy Spirit is the great teacher of human spirits: he taught Bezaleel and the skilled craftsmen in the wilderness how to make the fine linen and the gold and carved work for the tabernacle. All arts and sciences are perfectly known to him, and infinitely more than men can ever discover.

Yet he will not use these things in this holy controversy. In the quarrel of his covenant he uses neither philosophy, nor science, nor rhetoric. In contending against the powers of darkness, 'The sword of the Spirit is the Word of God.' 'It is written' (Matt. 4:4,7,10) is his master stroke. Words which God has spoken by holy men of old, and has caused to be recorded on the sacred page — these are the battle-axe and weapons of war of his Spirit. This book contains the Word of God, and is the

Word of God; and the Holy Spirit judges this book to be so effectual a weapon against evil that he uses this, and only this, as his sword in the great conflict with the powers of darkness.

The Word is the sword of the Spirit because it is of his own making. He will not use a weapon of human workmanship, lest the sword boast itself against the hand that wields it. The Holy Spirit revealed the mind of God to the minds of holy men. He spoke the word into their hearts, and thus he made them think as he would have them think and to write what he willed them to write; so that what they spoke and wrote was spoken and written as they were moved by the Holy Spirit. Blessed is the Holy Spirit for deigning to use so many writers, and yet to remain himself the veritable author of this collection of holy books. We are grateful for Moses, for David, for Isaiah, for Paul, for Peter, for John, but most of all for that superintending editor, that innermost author of the whole sacred volume — even the Holy Spirit.

A warrior may well be careful as to the make of his sword. If a man had made his own sword, had tempered the metal, had himself passed the blade through many fires, and wrought it to perfection, then, if he were a skilful workman, he would feel confidence in his sword. When work is done nowadays, it is, as a rule, badly done. Work done by contract is usually skimped in some part or another; but when a man does a work for himself he is likely to do it thoroughly and produce an article which he can depend upon. The Holy Spirit has made this book himself. Every portion of it bears his initial and impression; and thus he has a sword worthy of his own hand, a true 'Jerusalem blade'[1] of heavenly fabric. He delights to use a weapon so divinely made, and he uses it gloriously.

The Word of God is also the sword of the Spirit because he puts the edge upon it. It is because he is in it that it is so keen and cutting. I believe in the inspiration of holy Scripture, not only in the day when it was written, but onward, and even to this day. It is still inspired; the Holy Spirit still breathes through the chosen words. I told you the sword was all edge, but I would add that the Holy Spirit makes it so. It would have no edge at all if it were not for his presence within it, and his perpetual working by it. How many people read their Bibles, and yet derive no more benefit from the words than if they had read an old almanac! In fact, they would more easily keep awake over an ancient Bradshaw[2] than over a chapter of Scripture. The ministers of the gospel may preach God's Word in all sincerity and purity, and yet, if the Spirit of God is not present, we might as well have preached mere moral essays, for no good can come of our testimony.

The Holy Spirit rides in the chariot of Scripture, and not in the wagon of modern thought. Scripture is that ark of the covenant which contains the golden pot of manna, and also bears above it the divine light of God's shining. The Spirit of God works in, by, through, and with the Word; and if we keep to that Word, we may rest assured that the Holy Spirit will keep with us, and make our testimony to be a thing of power. Let us entreat the blessed Spirit to put an edge on our preaching, lest we say much and accomplish little. Hear us in this thing, oh blessed One!

The Word of God is the sword of the Spirit because he alone can instruct us in the use of it. You think, young man, that you can pick up your Bible, and go and preach from it at once, properly and successfully. You have made a presumptuous mistake. A sword is a weapon which may do hurt to the man who flourishes with it in mere wanton pride. No one can handle the sword of the Spirit properly except the chosen man whom God has ordained from before the foundation of the world and trained in feats of arms.

The elect of God are known by this: they love the Word of God, and they have a reverence for it, and discern between it and the words of man. Notice the lambs in the field. There may be a thousand ewes and lambs, but every lamb finds out its own mother. In the same way, a true-born child of God knows where to go for the milk which is to nourish his soul. The sheep of

Christ know the Shepherd's voice in the Word, and they will not follow a stranger, for they do not know the voice of strangers.

God's own people have discernment to discover and relish God's own Word. They will not be misled by the cunning craftiness of human devices. Saints know the Scriptures by inward instinct. The holy life, which God has infused into believers by his Spirit, loves the Scriptures, and learns how to use them for holy purposes. Young soldier, you must go to the training-ground of the Holy Spirit to be made a proficient swordsman. You will go in vain to the metaphysical philosopher or to the logician; for neither of these knows how to handle a spiritual weapon. In other areas they may be masters; but in the sacred use of divine theology they are mere fools. In the things of the Word we are dunces till we enter the school of the Holy Spirit. He must take the things of Christ, and show them to us. He must teach us how to grip this sword by faith, and how to hold it by watchfulness, so as to parry the adversary's thrust and carry the war into the foeman's territory.

He is well taught who can swing this great two-handed sword to and fro, and mow a lane through the midst of his opponents, and come out a conqueror at the end. It may take a long time to learn this art; but we have a skilful teacher. Those of us who have been in this warfare thirty or forty years feel that we have not yet reached the full use of this sword; no, I know for one, that I need daily to be taught how to use this mysterious weapon, which is capable of so much more than I have yet supposed. It is the sword of the Spirit, adapted for the use of an almighty arm, and therefore equal to the doing of far more than we think. Holy Spirit, teach us now feats of arms by this your sword!

But, chiefly, it is the sword of the Spirit, because he is the great Master in the use of it. Oh, that he would come and show us today how he can thrust and cleave with it! In this house of prayer we have often seen him at his work. Here the slain of the Lord have been many. We have seen this sword take off the head of many a Goliath doubt, and slay a horde of cares and unbeliefs. We have seen the Spirit pile up heaps of the slain when the Word of conviction has gone forth, and men have seen sin to be sin and fallen down as dead before the Lord and his law. We also know what the use of the sword by the Spirit of God means, for within our own being he has left marks of his prowess. He has killed our doubts and fears, and left no more misgivings to worry us.

There was a man of God[3] who was frequently subject to doubts, even doubts upon the fundamentals of religion. He hated this state of mind, but still he could not get rid of the habit of evil questioning. In answer to prayer, the Spirit came, and convinced him of the pride of his intellect, and of the wickedness of setting up his judgement against the Word of the Lord; and from that day forward he was never the subject of another fit of unbelief. He saw things clearly in the light of the Holy Spirit, and that is to see them indeed.

The great giant of doubt is sorely wounded by the sword of the Spirit — yes, he is slain outright; for the Spirit works in the believer such a conviction of the truth that assurance banishes suspicion. When the Holy Spirit deals with the lusts of the flesh, the lusts of the eye, and the pride of life, these also lie at his feet, trophies to the power of his mighty weapon, even the Word of God! The Holy Spirit is glorious in the use of this sword. He finds that this weapon suits his hand, and he seeks no other. Let us use it also, and be glad to do so. Though it is the sword of the Spirit, still our feebler hand may grasp it; yes, and find in the grasping that something of the divine power comes to our arm.

Dear brothers, is it not a very high honour put upon you, as soldiers of the cross, that you should be allowed — no, commanded — to take the sword of the Spirit? The raw recruit is not trusted with the general's sword, but here you are, armed with the weapon of God the Holy Spirit, and called upon to bear that sacred sword which is so gloriously wielded by the Lord God himself. This we are to bear, and no other.

Does the timid heart enquire, 'My Master, with what shall I meet my adversaries?' 'Here,' says the Holy Spirit, 'take this! This is my own sword; I have done great marvels with it; take it, and nothing shall stand against you.' When you remember the potency of this sword, when the Spirit tests it upon yourself, you may take it with confidence, and use it in your holy war with full assurance. That Word of God which could convert you, can convert anybody. If it could kill your despair, it can remove another man's despondency. If it has conquered your pride and self-will, it can subdue the like in your children and your neighbours. Having done what it has certainly done for you, you may be fully persuaded that, before its power, no case is hopeless. Therefore, see to it that from this day forward you use no other weapon than the sword of the Spirit, which is the Word of God.

2. Make the Word of God our own sword

This fairly lands me in the second portion of my discourse. The Word of God is the sword of the Spirit; but it is also to be *our* sword. Here I must begin again, and go over much of the same ground.

We will need a sword. Our warfare is not child's play: we mean business. We have to deal with fierce foes who are only to be met with keen weapons. Buffets will not suffice in this contest; we must come to sword-cuts. You may be of a very quiet spirit, but your adversaries are not so. If you attempt to play at Christian warfare, they will not. To meet the powers of darkness is no sham battle. They mean mischief. Nothing but your eternal damnation will satisfy the fiendish hearts of Satan and his crew.

You must take not so much a flag to unfurl, or a drum to beat, as a sword to use, and a particularly sharp sword too. In this combat you will have to use a sword that even evil spirits can feel, capable of dividing asunder soul and spirit, joints and marrow. If you are to live through this fight, and come off victorious, no form of conflict less sharp and cutting than sword-work will suffice. Depend upon it that in this struggle you will be forced to come to close quarters. The foe aims at your heart and pushes home. A spear will not do, nor bow and arrow; the enemy is too near for anything but hand-to-hand fighting.

Brothers, our foes are not only of our house, but also of our heart. I find an enemy within which is always near, and I cannot get away from him. I find that my antagonist will get his hand on my throat if he can. If our foes were far away, and we could play upon them with artillery which would kill at six or seven miles' distance, we might lead a pretty easy life. But no; they are here! They are at our doors! Yes, they are within us, nearer than hands and feet. Now for the short sword, the claymore of holy Scripture, to stab and cut, here and now. No sling and stone will avail us here, but we must take the sword. You have to slay your foe, or your foe will slay you. It is with us Christians as it was with the Highlanders in battle, when their leader called out to them, 'Lads, there they are! If you dinna kill them, they will kill you.' There is no room for peace; it is war to the knife, not only now, but to life's end.

The use of the sword is needful for attack. I have reminded you several times already that it will not suffice for the Christian to guard against sin and ward off temptation from himself; he has to assail the powers of evil. In our case, the best method of defence is an attack.

I have heard of one who would bring an action in law to gain his ends, for he thought this better than being the defendant. That may be a matter of question, but in war it is often safer to assail than defend. Carry the warfare into the enemy's territory. Be trying to win from the adversary, and he will not win so much from you. Do not merely be sober yourselves, but attack drunkenness. Do not be content with being free from superstition yourself, but expose it wherever it appears. Do not merely be devout when you feel obliged to be so, but pray for the growth of the kingdom; pray always. Do not merely say, 'I will keep Satan out of my family by bringing up my children properly', but go to the Sunday school, and teach other children, and so carry the war over the border.

God forbid that we should ever go to war as a nation! But if we were at war with some nation on the Continent, I would certainly say, 'Let the continentals have the battles on their own ground; we do not want a campaign over here.' It is wise to keep the war in the enemy's own regions. If we had fought the devil more in the world, he might never have been able to invade the church as terribly as he has done.

Attack with the sword, for it is your calling, and thus will you best defend yourself. We need the sword for real fighting. Do you think that you can dream yourselves into heaven, or ride there in the chariot of ease? Or fly on the wings of brass music? You make a great mistake if you imagine these things. A real war is raging, your opponents are in deadly earnest, and you must take your sword.

And, further, we need *this* sword: this sword of the Spirit, which is the Word of God. We say with David, 'There is none like that; give it to me' (1 Sam. 21:9). It has wrought such wonders that we prefer it to all others. No other will match the enemy's weapon. If we fight the devil with human reason, the first time our wooden sword comes in contact with a satanic temptation it will be cut in pieces. If you do not wield a true Jerusalem blade you are in grave peril; your weapon will break off at the hilt, and where will you be? Standing defenceless, with nothing but the handle of a broken sword in your hand, you will be the object of your adversary's ridicule. You must have this sword, for no other will penetrate the foe, and no other will last out the battle. After twenty years, what has become of the pious resolutions of your youth? What is the staying power of your consecration made in the hour of enthusiasm? Alas, how little trust can be placed in it! What would become of us after thirty years of fighting, if we did not have the Word of God to rely upon? The Word of the Lord endures for ever, but nothing else does. We may do well in early days, but we shall fail in old age if we do not have eternal truths to fall back upon.

I can commend this sword to you all, my brethren, although you are so varied in character. This sword suits every hand. Youth or age may alike use this weapon. These dear girls from the Orphanage[4] and yonder lads from the Bible-class may fight the battle of their youth with the Word of God; for holy Scripture may impress and guide our freshest life. You that have grown grey, you that have passed seventy or eighty, you will value the Bible more than ever, and you will find that this sword is the best for veteran warriors. Young men and young women, here is a sword suited for all of you, and well does it become the hand of the feeblest and the gentlest. The Holy Spirit has in the sacred Word prepared an implement of warfare suited for great minds and small, for the cultured and the uneducated. A wonderful sword this is, which, in the hand of faith, reveals an adaptation marvellous to the last degree.

Whatever others may say, it is sufficient for us that this is the regulation sword. A soldier is not left to choose his own equipment; he must carry such arms as his sovereign appoints. This is the regulation sword in Christ's army. The sword of the Spirit, which is the Word of God, is what you are bidden to take; and if you in wilfulness resolve to exchange it for another, you commit an act of rebellion, and you make the change at your own risk and peril. Come, then, let each one of us take the Word of God, and carry it nearer our hearts than ever; for such is the word of command, 'Take the sword of the Spirit, which is the word of God.'

Now, see what we are told to do. We need a sword; we need *this* sword; we are to *take* this sword. Note that we are not told that we may lay it down. The demand to take the sword is continuous, and there is no hint of its being suspended. There is a time, of course, when the soldier of her Majesty may remove his sword from his side, and put off his regimentals; there is never such a time with a Christian.

One might have thought, from what we have seen recently, that orders had come from headquarters that the soldiers were to lay down the sword of the Spirit, the Word of God, and take to lighter weapons. Entertainments, amusements, farces, and sing-song are now used to do what the gospel has failed to achieve! Sadly, is it not so? Well, if any will try these silly toys, I can only say that they have no command from their Lord to warrant them in their proceedings. Take all these things, and see what they will do; but you make the trial at your own risk, and on your own heads the result of failure will fall.

The standing orders are to take the sword of the Spirit, and no new regulation has ever been issued by the great captain of salvation. From the days of Paul till now, the word stands: 'Take the sword of the Spirit.' All other things will surely fail, and hence the one sole abiding command is, 'Take the sword of the Spirit.' We are not told to hang up this sword for exhibition. Certain people have a handsomely bound Bible to lay upon the table of the best room, and a fine ornament it is. A family Bible is a treasure. But I urge you, do not let your love of the Bible end there. With a soldier in war, a sword is not meant to be hung up in the tent, nor even to be flourished in the air; but it is issued to be used.

Nor are we to push this sword into a sheath, as many do who take the Bible and add so much of criticism or of their own opinion to it that its edge is not felt. Many men use their low opinion of inspiration as a scabbard into which they push the Bible down. Their vast knowledge makes a beautiful scabbard, and they push down the sword, saying, 'Keep still there! Oh, sword of the Lord, rest and be quiet!' After we have preached our heart out, and men have felt the power of it, they make a desperate effort to imprison the Word in their unbelieving theory, or in their worldliness. They hold down the Word all the week with a firm hand, for fear its edge or point should wound them. It is the scabbard of culture, or philosophy, or of progress, and in this they shut up the living Word of God as in a coffin.

We are not to bury the Word under other matters; but we are to take it as a sword, which means, as I understand it, first, *believe* it. Believe every portion of it; believe it with a true and real faith, not with a mere credal faith, which says, 'This is the orthodox thing.' Believe it as a matter of fact for every day, affecting your life. Believe it.

And when you have believed it, then *study* it. Oh, for a closer study of the Word of God! Are there not some of you who have never even heard or read all that the Lord has said? Are there not passages of the Bible which you have never read? It is a melancholy fact that there should be even a line of the sacred Scriptures which has never once come under your eye. Do read the Bible right through, from beginning to end. Begin tomorrow: no, begin today, and go steadily through the whole of the sacred books, with prayer and meditation. Never let it be suspected that God has recorded truths in his Word which you have never even once read.

Study the Word, and work out its meaning. Go deep into the Spirit of inspiration. He gets most gold who digs the deepest in this mine. They used to say of certain mines in Cornwall that the deeper you went the richer was the ore; assuredly is it so with the mines of inspired Scripture. The deeper you go under the Spirit's guidance, the larger the reward is for your toil.

Take the sword with the grip of sincere faith; hold it fast by a fuller knowledge, and then exercise yourself daily in its use. The sword is to be taken for earnest fight. You will not be long before occasion arises in such a world as this. You will have to parry with it, to pierce with it, to cut with it, and to kill with it.

'Where shall I begin?' says one. Begin at home, and, for many days, you will have your hands full. When you have slain all the rebels at home, and long before that, you may take a turn at those around you in the world, and in the professing church. Inside your own heart you will find a band of bandits which should be exterminated. There will always be need to keep the sword going within your own territory. End this civil war before you go into foreign parts. When the war within the city of Mansoul[5] has been victoriously carried through, besiege the heart of your friend, your child, your neighbour. Behold, the world lies in the wicked one! Errors abound, and colossal systems of falsehood still stand aloft. Men are still dragged down by the arch-deceiver. Surely, we feel our swords flying out of their sheaths when we think of the millions who are being ruined by sin and error. Oh, for a mighty onslaught upon the powers of darkness!

Once more, we are to take this sword with a purpose. We are to use it that we may be able to stand and to withstand. If you want to stand, draw the sword and smite your doubts. How fiercely unbelief assails! Here comes a doubt as to your election. Pierce it through with the Word. Here comes a doubt as to the precious blood. Cleave it from head to foot with the assurance of the Word that the blood of Jesus cleanses us from all sin. Here comes another doubt, and yet another. As quick as arm can move, drive texts of Scripture through every new fallacy, every new denial of truth, and spit the whole of them upon the rapier of the Word. It will be for your good to kill these doubts outright. Do not play with them, but fight them in real earnest.

You will find that temptations also will come in hordes. Meet them with the precepts of sacred Writ, and slay even the desire of evil by the Spirit's application of the Holy Word. The washing of water by the Word is a glorious cleanser. Discouragements will arise like mists of the morning. Oh, that God's Word may shine them away with the beams of the promises! Your afflictions multiply, and you will never be able to overcome impatience and distrust except by the infallible Word of God. You can bear trial, and bear it patiently, if you use this weapon to kill anxiety. You will 'stand fast in the evil day', and having done all, you will still stand, if this sword is in your hand.

You have not only to stand fast yourselves, but you have to win souls for Christ. Do not try to conquer sin in others, or capture a heart for Jesus, except with the sword of the Spirit. How the devil laughs when we try to make converts apart from holy Scripture and the Holy Spirit! He laughs, I say; for he derides our folly. What can you do, you children, playing with your little wooden swords — what can you do against men covered from head to foot with the steel mail of the habit of sin? Sunday-school teachers, teach your children more and more the pure Word of God; and preachers, do not try to be original, but be content to take of the things of Christ and show them to the people; for that is what the Holy Spirit himself does; and you will be wise to use his method and his sword. No sinner around you will be saved except by the knowledge of the great truths contained in the Word of God. No man will ever be brought to repentance, to faith, and to life in Christ, apart from the constant application of the truth through the Spirit.

I hear great shouting, great noises everywhere, about great things that are going to be done; let us see them. The whole world is going to be embraced within the church, so they say. I fear the world will not be much the better for inclusion in such a church. Big boasters should heed the word of the wise man, 'Let not the one who puts on his armour boast like the one who takes it off' (1 Kings 20:11). If the champion goes forth with any other sword than the Word of God, he had better not boast at all; for he will come back with his sword broken, his shield cast away, and himself grimy with dishonour. Defeat awaits that man who forsakes the Word of the Lord.

I will have finished when I have asked you to remember that the text is in the present tense. Take to yourself the sword of the Spirit even now. Believers have all sorts of perils; let each of them take the sword of the Spirit, and they will overcome every foe. Here, too, are seekers who wish to be Christians, but they cannot compass it. What is the matter? 'Oh,' says one, 'I have been in the habit of sinning, and the habit is very strong upon me.' Fight sinful habits with the Word of God, as the sword of the Spirit; only in this way will you conquer your evil self. Find a text of Scripture that will cleave your sin down to the spine, or stab it to the heart. 'Alas! Satan tempts me horribly,' cries one; 'I have been assailed lately in many ways.' Have you? You are not the first.

Our divine Lord in the wilderness was tempted by the devil. He might have fought Satan with a thousand weapons, but he chose to defeat him with this one only. He said, 'It is written; it is written; it is written.' He pricked the foeman so sorely with this sharp point, that the arch-adversary thought to try the same sword, and he also began to say, 'It is written.' But he cut himself with this sword, for he did not quote the passages correctly, nor give the whole of them, and the Master soon found the way to knock aside his sword, and wound him still more. Follow your Lord's example.

'Oh,' says one, 'I am so low in spirits.' Very well; fight lowness of spirits with the Word of God. 'The doctor recommended,' says one, 'that I take a little spirits to raise my spirits.' Those doctors are always having this sin laid to their charge. I am not so sure that they are not often maligned. You like the dose, and that is why you take it.

Try the Word of God for lowness of spirits, and you will have found a sure remedy. I find, if I can lay a promise under my tongue, like a sweet lozenge, and keep it in my mouth or mind all the day long, I am happy enough. If I cannot find a Scripture to comfort me, then my inward troubles are multiplied. Fight despondency and despair with the sword of the Spirit.

I cannot tell what your particular difficulty may be at this moment, but I give you this direction for all holy warfare: 'Take the sword of the Spirit, which is the word of God.' You must overcome every enemy, and this weapon is all you need.

If you would overcome sin and conquer unbelief, take a word such as this: 'Look to me, and be saved, all you ends of the earth' (Isa. 45:22)[6], and as you look you shall be saved, and doubt shall die, and sin be slain. God grant you his Spirit's aid, for Christ's sake! Amen.

The Word and the Spirit

Chapter 7

Search the Scriptures

When men will not learn of God, how huge their folly grows! ... Not caring to have God in their hearts, forsaking the living fountain, they have hewn out to themselves cisterns which are broken and hold no water.

7.
Search the Scriptures

To the law and to the testimony! If they do not speak according to this word, it is because there is no light in them — Isa. 8:20

A sermon delivered on Lord's Day morning, 17 January 1858, by C. H. Spurgeon at the Music Hall, Royal Surrey Gardens. Sermon No. 172

When men will not learn of God, how huge their folly grows! If they despise the wisdom that is from above, how grievously does God allow them to prove their own ignorance! When a man will not bow down before God the Most High, immediately he builds for himself an idol; he makes an image of wood or stone, and he degrades himself by bowing before the work of his own hands. When men will not receive the Scripture testimony concerning God's creation, immediately they begin to form theories that are a thousand times more ridiculous than they have ever endeavoured to make the Bible account of it; for God leaves them, if they will not accept his solution of the problem, to grope for another, and their own solution is so absurd that all the world except themselves has sense enough to laugh at it. And when men leave the sacred book of revelation — Ah! My friends, where do they go? We find that in Isaiah's time they went to strange places; for he says in the 19th verse that they sought mediums and wizards, who whisper and mutter; yes, they sought among the dead for things concerning the living and became the dupes of necromancers.

It is extraordinary that the men who most of all rail at faith are remarkable for credulity. One of the greatest unbelievers in the world, who has called himself a free-thinker from his birth, is to be found now tottering into his tomb, believing the most absurd nonsense, which even a child might refute. Not caring to have God in their hearts, forsaking the living fountain, they have hewn out to themselves cisterns which are broken and hold no water. Oh, that each of us may be wiser, that we may not forsake the good old path, nor leave the way that God has prepared for us! If we despise the guidance of an unerring Father, what wonder that we should travel among thorns and briars and tear our own flesh, or worse than that, fall among dark mountains, and be lost among the chasms there. Seek in the word of God and read, 'Search the Scriptures, for in them you think you have eternal life; and these are they which testify of' Jesus Christ (John 5:39).

I feel that, at this particular crisis of religious affairs, it is imperative upon the Christian minister to urge his people to hold fast the doctrines of the truth — the words of God. This seems likely to become the age of preaching, rather than the age of praying. We now see everywhere large congregations assembling in halls and abbeys to listen to the Word preached, and it is an ominous sign of the times that these preachings are not only now espoused by the orthodox, but even by those whom we have considered to be at least somewhat heretical from the old faith of the Protestant church.

It becomes, therefore, a serious thing; for it is most probable — and may not every wise man see it? — that whoever may now arise who has some powers of oratory and some graces of eloquence, will be likely to attract the multitude, preach he what he may, though the word that he should utter be as false as God's Word is true, and as contrary to the gospel as hell is opposed to heaven. Does it not seem probable that in this age he would attract a multitude of followers? And is it not also very likely that through that spurious charity which is now growing upon us, which would gag the mouths of honest reprovers, we will find it hard to rebuke the impostor when he arises, and difficult to expose the falsehood, even though it may be apparent to us?

We are now happily so well mingled together, the Dissenter and the Churchman have now become so friendly with each other, that we have less cause to dread the effects of bigotry than the effects of latitudinarianism.[1] We have some reason now to be upon the watchtower, lest some should happen to arise in our midst, the spurious offspring of these happy times of evangelical alliance, who will claim our charity, while they are preaching that which we in our hearts do totally condemn.

And what better advice can the minister give in such times as these? To what book will he commend his hearers? How will he keep them fast? Where is the anchor which he will give them to cast into the rocks? Or where are the rocks into which they should cast their anchor? Our text is a solution to that question. We are here furnished with a great answer to the inquiry: 'To the law and to the testimony! If they speak not according to this word, it is because there is no light in them.'

First, I shall endeavour to urge you to bring certain things, to which we are afraid a superstitious importance may be attached, 'To the law and to the testimony.' Secondly, I shall try to show the good effects that will follow if each of you rigidly brings everything you hear and believe 'To the law and to the testimony.' And, thirdly, I shall give you some powerful reasons why you should subject everything to this sacred touchstone; and close by offering you some advice how you may do this truly and profitably.

1. Bringing doctrines, ideas and thoughts to the test of God's Word

Permit me to urge you to bring certain things 'To the law and to the testimony.' First, I would have you bring to the test of the book of God the ideas engendered in you by your early training. It is very much the custom of people to say, 'Was I not born in the Church of England? Ought I not therefore to continue in it?' Or, on the other hand, 'Was not my grandmother an Immersionist? Ought not I therefore, to continue in the Baptist denomination?' God forbid that I should say anything against your venerable and pious relatives; or that you should pay any disrespect to their teaching! We always respect their advice, even when we cannot receive it, for the sake of the person who offers it to us; knowing that their training, even should it have been mistaken, was nevertheless well meant.

But we claim for ourselves, as men, that we should not be fed with doctrines as we were fed in our helpless infancy, with food chosen for us. We claim that we should have the right of judging whether the things which we have received and heard are according to this sacred book; and if we find that in any way our training has been erroneous, we do not consider that we are violating any principle of affection, if we dare to come forth from our families, and join a denomination holding tenets far different from those which our parents had espoused.[2]

Let us each recollect that, as God has given every man a head on his shoulders, every man is bound to use his own head, and not his father's. God gave your father judgement. Well and good; he judged for himself. God has given you a judgement; judge for yourself too. Say, concerning all that you have received in your early childhood, 'Well, I will not lightly part with this, for it may be sterling gold; but at the same time, I will not blindly hoard it, for it may be counterfeit coin. I will sit down to the study of the sacred book, and I will endeavour, as far as I can, to unprejudice myself. I will read the Bible, just as if I had never heard any preacher, or had never been taught by a parent, and I will then endeavour to find out what God says; and what God says, be it what it may, I will believe and espouse, hoping that by his grace I may also feel the power of it in my own soul.'

Remember, also, to bring the preachers of the gospel to this standard. A great many of you know very little about what gospel is. The general notion is that every one of us is right; that though today I may contradict someone else, and someone else may contradict me, yet we are all right; and though it is treason to common sense to believe such a thing, still this is a common idea.

Some men always believe like the last speaker. Should they hear the most hyper of hyper-Calvinists, they believe with him the fullness of the doctrine of reprobation. Should they hear the next day the most extreme Arminian, they believe with him the most universal of redemptions and the most powerful of free wills. Should they then hear the genuine Calvinist, who preaches that man has destroyed himself, but in God is his help found, perhaps then they think this man contradicts himself, and for once they rebel against their teachers. But it is probable that should they hear such a person again, they will be easily reconciled to seeming contradictions; for to them it is just the man's appearance, just the man's way of saying the thing, that they like, and not the thing that he says.

I have heard of holy Mr Durham,[3] the writer of that sweet book on Solomon's Song. If I had lived in his time, I think that I should never have wanted to hear any other preacher; I would have sat, both by night and day, to receive the sweet droppings of his honied lips. But in his time there was a young preacher,[4] whose name is totally forgotten, whose church was crowded to the door while Mr Durham's meeting house nearby was forsaken. The reason for that is because the mass of people do not lay hold upon *what* is said, but upon *how* it is said. If it is said smartly, said prettily, and said forcibly, that is enough for them, though it is a lie; but if the truth is spoken, they will not receive it unless it is attended by some graces of oratory and eloquence. Now, the Christian that has got above his babyhood does not care about how the man says it; it is the thing that is said that he cares about. All he asks is, 'Did he speak the truth?' He just gets hold of the core. To him the straw is nothing, and the chaff less. He does not care for the trimming of the feast nor for the exquisite workmanship of the dish; he only cares for that which is solid food for himself.

Now, my dear friends, I claim for myself, when I enter this pulpit, the right of being heard, but I do not claim the right of being believed, unless the words that I speak should be in accordance with this sacred book. I desire you to serve me as I would have you serve everybody else — bring us each 'To the law and to the testimony.' I thank God that I have no need to be ashamed of my Bible. I sometimes am ashamed of this translation of it, when I see how, in some important points, it is not true to God's Word; but of God's own Word I can say that it is the man of my right hand, my meditation both day and night, and if there is anything I preach that is contrary to this Word, trample it in the mire, spit upon it, and despise it. The truth lies here. It is not what I say, but what my God says, that you are commanded to receive. Put me and put all my brethren into the sieve; cast us each into the fire, put us into the crucible of truth, and what is not according to God's Word must be consumed like dross.

There is another class of men quite contrary to those I have referred to; these men are their own preachers. They believe no one but themselves, and without knowing it, there is every reason for them to hate the Pope, because 'two of a trade never agree', they being popes themselves. These people, if they hear a truth preached, do not judge it by the Bible, but by what they think the truth ought to be.

I have heard a person say, for instance, when he has heard the doctrine of election, or of particular redemption, 'Well, now, the doctrine does not please me; I do not like it.' And then he begins to urge some objection which he has forged upon his own anvil, yet never trying to quote a Scripture text to refute it, if he can; never turning to some old saying of the Prophets and endeavouring to find out that the doctrine was an error, but only judging of it by his own opinion, by his wishes as to what the truth ought to be.

What would you think of a man who were to say to an astronomer, 'Now, it is of no use your telling me that the constellation of Scorpio is of such-and-such a shape; I tell you, I do not like the look of it. My dear fellow, I don't think that the constellation of Scorpio ought to have been made that shape, and I think this star ought to have been put just here instead of there, and then all would be well.' The astronomer would simply smile at him, and say, 'Your opinion does not signify, because it does not alter facts. If you think I am wrong, your right way to disprove me is not to say where you think the stars ought to be, but just come and take a look through my telescope and see where the stars are.'

Now it is just the same with the truth. People say, 'I do not like such a truth.' That is no refutation of it. The question is, 'Is it in the Bible?' Because if it is there, like it or not like it, it is a fact, and all the minister has to do is to report the facts that he finds there. Why, the astronomer cannot put the stars in a row, like a row of gaslights, to please you, and the minister cannot put the doctrines into a shape in which you would wish to have them cast. All the astronomer does is to map them out and say, 'That is how they are in the sky.' You must then look at the sky and see whether it is so.

All I have to do is to tell you what I find in the Bible. Remember, if you do not like it, that is no refutation of it, nor do I care for your liking it or not liking it. The only thing is, is it in the Bible? If it is there I shall not stop to prove it; I do not come here to prove a doctrine at all. If it is in the Bible, it is true: there it is; I tell it out. Reject it, and you do so to your own condemnation; for you yourself believe the Bible to be true, and I prove it to be there, and therefore it must be true.

Should it be according to your mind? Would you like to have a Bible made for the devices of your own heart? If it were, it would be a worthless thing. Would you desire to have a gospel according to your wishes? Then with some of you it would be a gospel that allowed lasciviousness. Would you wish to have a revelation made that should pamper you in your lusts and indulge you in your pride? If so, know this: God will never stoop to feed your haughtiness or wantonness. The Bible is a God-like book; he demands your faith in it; and though you kick against it, this stone can never be broken. Mind you, you may be broken upon it; yes, it may fall upon you and bruise you to powder. I urge you, then, bring your own thoughts and your own sentiments to the touchstone of the truth, for 'If they speak not according to this word, it is because there is no light in them.'

And just do the same with all books that you read. This is the age of book-making and book-writing. Nowadays, what with periodical literature and the books upon our shelves, our Bibles do not get read much. I will tell you a truthful story as it was told to me. There was a young man, who is now a student for the ministry, who was so extraordinarily ignorant of his own Bible, that upon hearing a young minister mention the story of Nebuchadnezzar's being driven out from men, until his nails grew like birds' claws, and his hair like eagles' feathers, he said to the minister at the close of the sermon, 'Well, that was a queer story you told the people, certainly. Where did you fish that up?' 'Why,' said the minister, 'have you never read your Bible? Can you not find it in the book of Daniel?' The young man had read a great many other things, but had never read his Bible through, and yet was going to be a teacher of it!

Now, I fear that the same ignorance is very current in many people. They do not know what is in the Bible. They could tell you what is in the *Churchman's Penny* or the *Christian's Penny* or the *Churchman's Magazine* or the *Wesleyan Magazine* or the *Baptist Magazine* or the *Evangelical Magazine* and all that; but there is one old magazine, a magazine of arms, a magazine of wealth, that they forget to read — that old-fashioned book called the Bible.

'Ah!' said one who had been a great classic, when he came to die, 'I would to God I had spent as much time in reading my Bible as I have spent in reading Livy![5] I would to God I had been as exact in my criticisms of holy Scripture as I was in criticisms upon Horace!'[6] Oh, that we were wise, to give the Bible the largest share of our time, and ever to continue reading it, both by day and night, that we might be as trees planted by the rivers of water, bringing forth our fruit in our season!

Let us remember, as ministers of the gospel, what McCheyne[7] beautifully said: 'Depend upon it; it is God's Word, not man's comment upon God's Word, that saves souls.' I have noticed, that if ever we have a conversion at any time, in ninety-nine cases out of a hundred, the conversion is rather traceable to the text, or to some Scripture quoted in the sermon, than to any trite or original saying by the preacher. It is God's Word that breaks the fetters and sets the prisoner free. It is God's Word instrumentally that saves souls, and therefore let us bring everything to the touchstone: 'To the law and to the testimony; if they speak not according to this word, it is because there is no light in them.'

2. Good effects of careful study

Now I pass to my second point. Brothers, let me show you some of the good effects that you will derive from a minute and careful study of the law and testimony of God. First, remember that unless you study the Word of God, you will not be competent to detect error. A man may, in your hearing, preach downright falsehood, but you will not be qualified to judge concerning that falsehood unless you have studied the Word of God.

You and I would not be fit to sit on the judgement bench of some of the superior courts of our land, because we are not acquainted with the intricacies of the law. We could not quote precedents, for we have not been taught them. And so no man is able to judge concerning the thing that he hears, unless he is able to quote Scripture — unless he understands the Word of God and is able to perceive and to know what it means.

I hear someone say that the Bible is so difficult a book that he is sure he never could understand it. Mind you, man, the Bible is so plain a book that he that is willing to understand it may do so; it is so plain that he that runs may read, and read while he runs; yes, it is so plain, that the simpler a man is, the more easily he can understand it. All the learning that man ever received is more a hindrance than a benefit when he comes for the first time to read the Word. Learning may untie many a knot afterwards, it may unravel many a mystery in later times; but we have heard deep-minded critics say that at first they would have given all the world, if they could have thrown their learning aside, just to read the Bible as the humble cottager reads it, and believe it as God's Word, without any quibbles of criticism.

Think of how Mrs Beecher Stowe[8] represents Uncle Tom reading it. He could not read it fast; so he just spelled it over letter by letter, and word by word; and the Bible is one of the books, she says, that always gains by that way of reading. He read it: 'Let — not — your — hearts — be —' and then he stopped at the long word, and he fumbled it out at last, and it was, 'troubled. You believe in God, believe also in me.' Why, it gets sweeter from your being a long time reading it; and so far from your lack of learning disqualifying you from understanding the Bible, the mass of it is all the more understandable from the simplicity of your heart. Come and search the Scriptures. They are no such mysterious fables or learned volumes of hard words as some men say. This is no closed book, as the priest would tell us; it is a volume which the Sunday-school child may understand, if the Spirit of God rests upon his heart. It is a book which the rough-handed workman may comprehend as well as the learned divine, and many have in this way gained great wisdom. I say again, read your Bibles, that you may be qualified to detect error.

But again I do not like a man who is always looking out for error. That man has got some error in his own heart, depend upon it. They say, 'Set a thief to catch a thief;' and it is very likely that there is some love of error in your heart, or else you would not be so ready to suspect it in other people.

But let me give you another reason. Search your Bibles; for then, when you are in a matter of dispute, you will be able to speak very confidently. There is nothing that gives a man so much power among his fellows as confidence. If in conversation I am contradicted as to any sentiment that I propound, if I have got Scripture at my fingers' ends — why, I laugh at my opponent, and though he may be ever so wise and have read ten times more books than I have ever seen, I just smile at him, if I can quote Scripture. Then I am confident — I am sure, I am certain about the matter — for 'Thus says the Lord' is an argument that no man can answer. It makes a man seem very foolish when he has to speak in a diffident manner.

I always think that certain elegant ministers, who are afraid of being called dogmatic, and who therefore propound the gospel as if they hardly liked to say they were sure it was true — as if they thought so, they nearly thought so — still they did not think so quite enough to say they knew, but leave it to their hearers. I always think they show the littleness of their minds in doing so. It may be a great thing to doubt, but it also is a great thing to hold your tongue while you are doubting, and not to open your mouth till you believe. Then, when you do open your mouth, say the thing you know is true, and stick to it, not as an opinion, but as an incontrovertible fact. No man will ever do much among his fellows till he can speak confidently what he knows to be revealed. Now, Bible readers, you can attain this confidence, but you can get it nowhere else but at the foot of Scripture.

Hear ministers alone, and you will be led to doubt, for one of them will confound what his brother sought to prove; but read your Bibles, and when you get the Word legible by its own light, impressed upon your own hearts by the Holy Spirit, then —

> Should all the forms that men devise,
> Assault your faith with treacherous art,
> You'll call them vanity and lies,
> And bind the gospel to your heart.

Furthermore, search the Scriptures, and bring everything you hear to this great test, because in doing so you will get a rich harvest of blessing to your own soul. I suppose there is scarcely a text in holy Scripture that has not been the instrument of the salvation of a soul. Now he that walks among wise men will be wise, and he that walks among the wise men that wrote holy Scripture stands at least the highest probability of being made wise unto salvation. If I desired to put myself into the most likely place for the Lord to meet with me, I should prefer the house of prayer; for it is in preaching that the Word is most blessed. But still I think I should equally desire the reading of the Scriptures, for I might pause over every verse, and say, 'Such a verse was blessed to so many souls; then why not to me? I am at least in the pool of Bethesda; I am walking among its porches, and who can tell but that the angel will stir the pool of the Word, while I lie helplessly by the side of it, waiting for the blessing?'

Yes, this truth is so great — that God has blessed every word of Scripture — that I remember a striking anecdote of the conversion of a man by a passage of Scripture that did not seem adapted for any such purpose. You know that chapter in Genesis, that very dull chapter, where we read, 'and Methuselah lived 969 years, and he died' (Genesis 5:27), and such a one lived so many years, 'and he died'? We have heard of its being read once in public, and a man who stood there when he heard the words often repeated — 'and he died' — thought, 'Ah! And I shall die!' And it was the first note of warning that had ever struck his seared conscience, and was the means under God of bringing him to Jesus.

Now, read the Scriptures for this reason: If you desire salvation, and if you are panting after mercy, if you feel your sin and want salvation, come to this sea of love, to this treasury of light, to this wardrobe of rich clothing, to this fountain of bliss; come and have your wants supplied out of the fullness of the riches of Jesus, who is 'evidently set forth' in this Word, 'crucified among you'.

3. The necessity of continued study of God's Word

And now let me endeavour, as briefly as I can, to urge upon you yet again the constant and perpetual reading of the Word of God, not only for the reasons that I have now propounded, but for others more important.

Many false prophets have gone forth into the world. I urge you, then, if you would not be led astray, be diligent in the study of the Word of God. In certain parts of Dr Livingstone's[9] travels, he tells us that his guides were either so ignorant, or so determined to deceive him, that he could have done far better without them than with them, and he constantly had to refer to his compass, lest he should be led astray. Now, I would not say a hard thing if I did not believe it to be true; but I do solemnly think that there are some professed teachers of the Word, who are either so ignorant of spiritual things in their own hearts, or else so determined to preach anything but Christ, that you might do better without them than with them. Hence you have an absolute necessity to turn perpetually to this great compass by which alone you can steer your way.

I scorn a charity that after all is not charity. I must tell you what I believe. Some would have me now stand and say, 'All that are eminent preachers are most certainly truthful preachers.' I cannot say it.

If at any time I hear a man preach the doctrine of justification by faith alone, through the merits of Christ, I give him my hand, and call him my brother, because he is right in the main thing. But when I do that I am a long way from endorsing many other of his sentiments. It may be that he denies the effectual power of the Spirit in conversion, it may be he does not hold the doctrine of the entire depravity of the human race, does not insist upon free sovereign grace, does not hold forth and teach the doctrine of substitution and satisfaction through Christ.

Now, I will not make such a fool of myself as to tell you that where that man differs from the Word of God he is true. No doubt that man may be blessed for your salvation. But there may be a curse upon his ministry notwithstanding, so that while you may be saved by it, you may be all your lifetime subject to bondage through it, and you may go groaning where you ought to have gone singing, crying where you might have had a sacred burst of joy. You sit under such-and-such a man who has been made the means of your conversion, but he tells you that your salvation depends upon yourself, and not upon the power of Christ. He insists upon it that you may, after all, fall from grace and be a castaway; he tells you that although you are saved, God did no more love you than he loved Judas; that there is no such thing as special love, no such thing, in fact, as election. He tells you that others might have come to Christ, as well as yourself — that there was no extraordinary power put out in your case, more than in any others. Well, if he does not lead you to glory in man, to magnify the flesh, and sometimes to trust in yourself, or else lead you to distress yourself where there is no need for distress, I should marvel indeed, inasmuch as his doctrine is false, and must mislead you. It may be the means of your salvation, yet it may fail in many points to minister to your edification and comfort. Therefore, if you would not be misled in this way, search the Scriptures.

There is a solemn danger of being absolutely misled. You may hear all that the minister says, but he may forget to tell you the vital part of the truth. He may be one who delights in ceremonies, but does not insist upon the grace therein. He may hold forth to you the rubric and sacrament, and tell you there is efficacy in obedience to the one, and attention to the other, and he may forget to tell you that unless a man is born again of the Spirit he cannot see the kingdom of God. Now, under such a ministry you may not only be misled, but alas! You may be destroyed altogether.

He may be one who insists much upon morality of life; he may tell you to be honest, just, and sober. But he may forget to tell you that there is a deeper work required than mere morality. He may film the surface over and never send the lancet into the deep ulcer of your heart's corruption. He may give you some palliating dose, some medicine that may still your conscience; he may never say to you, '"There is no peace," says my God, "for the wicked"' (Isa. 57:21).

He may be one of those that prophesies smooth things, that does not like to disturb you. Remember that your minister may be the instrument in the hands of Satan of blindfolding your eyes and leading you to hell, while all the while you thought you were going to heaven.

Ah, and hear me yet: I do not exclude myself from my own censure. It may be possible — I pray God it may not be so — that I myself may have mistaken the reading of holy Scripture, that I may have preached to you 'a different gospel which is not another' (Gal. 1:6-7), and therefore I demand of you that my own teaching, and the teaching of every other man, whether by pen or lip, should be always brought 'to the law and to the testimony', lest we should deceive you and lead you astray.

It would be an awful thing, if I should be the means of leading any of you into the gulf. Although in some measure your blood must be upon my head, if I deceive you, yet I urge you, remember that I am not further responsible for your souls than my power can carry me. If you are misled by me, after this solemn declaration of mine, you will be as truly guilty as if I had not misguided you. I charge you, as you love your own souls, as you would make sure work for eternity, put no more trust in me than you would in any other man, only so far as I can prove, by infallible testimony of God's Word, that what I have said is true. Stand always to this: 'To the law and to the testimony; if they do not speak according to this word, it is because there is no light in them.'

I heard a story once that I remember to have told before, of some young person going out of the place, and saying, 'Well, I don't like Mr Spurgeon at all; he is so high in doctrine; he said so-and-so.' And then the young body quoted a text out of the Bible as a very wicked thing that I had said — something about the potter having power over the clay. So the friend who was with her said, 'It was Paul said that, not Mr Spurgeon.' 'Ah!' said she, 'and I think the apostle Paul was a great deal too high too.'

Well, we are very glad to incur censure of that sort, and will not at all object to go with Paul wherever he may go; but we do entreat you never at any time to take our bare saying for a thing, but always to turn to your Bible and see whether it is so! Some Christian fathers have a good habit: when the boys and girls come home, they say 'Well, now, what was the text?' And then the father wants them to tell over what the minister has said, and even the small boy knows something, and tells something or other that the minister said from the pulpit. Then the father turns to his Bible to see whether these things be so. Then he endeavours to explain the hard things; so that they become like those noble Bereans, who were more noble than those of Thessalonica, because they searched the Scriptures, whether those things were so.

And now I may just hint at one or two distinctive doctrines[10] that I have always preached to you, specific doctrines that I desire you most anxiously to enquire into. Now, take nothing at second-hand from me, but try all of it by the written Word.

I believe and I teach that all men by nature are lost by Adam's fall.

See whether that is true or not. I hold that men have so gone astray that no man either will or can come to Christ except the Father draw him. If I am wrong, find me out.

I believe that God, before all worlds, chose to himself a people whom no man can number for whom the Saviour died, to whom the Holy Spirit is given, and who will infallibly be saved.

You may dislike that doctrine; I do not care. See if it is not in the Bible. See if it does not there declare that we are 'elect according to the foreknowledge of God the Father' (1 Peter 1:2) and so on.

I believe that every elect child of God must assuredly be brought by converting grace from the ruins of the fall, and must assuredly be 'kept by the power of God, through faith, for salvation' (1 Peter 1:5) beyond the hazard of ever totally falling away.

If I am wrong there, get out your Bibles, and refute me in your own houses.

I hold it to be a fact that every man who is converted will lead a holy life, and yet at the same time will put no dependence on his holy life, but trust only in the blood and righteousness of Jesus Christ.

And I hold that every man that believes is in duty bound to be immersed. I hold the baptism of infants to be a lie and a heresy, but I claim for that great ordinance of God, believer's baptism, that it should have the examination of Scripture. I hold that to none but believers may immersion be given, and that all believers are in duty bound to be immersed.

If I am wrong, well and good; do not believe me. But if I am right, obey the Word with reverence. I will have no error, even upon a point which some men think to be unimportant; for a grain of truth is a diamond, and a grain of error may be of serious consequence to us, to our injury and hurt.

I hold, then, that none but believers have any right to the Lord's Supper; that it is wrong to give the Lord's Supper indiscriminately to all, and that none but Christians have a right either to the doctrines, the benefits, or the ordinances of God's house.

If these things are not so, condemn me as you please; but if the Bible is with me, your condemnation is of no avail.

And now I charge you to read your Bibles, for one thing. Read your Bibles to know what the Bible says about *you*; and some of you, when you turn the pages over, will find the Bible says, 'You are poisoned by bitterness and bound by iniquity' (Acts 8:23). If that startles you, turn over another page, and read this verse: 'Come unto me, all you who labour and are heavy laden, and I will give you rest' (Matt. 11:28), and when you have read that, turn to another and read, 'Therefore, having been justified by faith, we have peace with God through our Lord Jesus Christ' (Rom. 5:1). I urge you, do not put away your Bibles for so long that their dust condemns you; but take them out, bend your knees, seek for the Spirit of divine teaching, and turn these pages with diligent search, and see if you can find there the salvation of your souls, through our Lord Jesus Christ. May the blessing of God rest upon you in doing so, through Jesus Christ. Amen.

Chapter 8

The church of God and the truth of God

This is a day of strife, a day of division, a time of war and fighting between professing Christians... The day is come when we must know who are for the Lord and for his truth, and who are on the side of error.

8.
The church of God and the truth of God

The house of God, which is the church of the living God, the pillar and ground of the truth — 1 Tim. 3:15

A sermon delivered on Lord's Day morning, 14 September 1856, by C. H. Spurgeon at New Park Street Chapel, Southwark, published on Thursday, 21 May 1908.
Sermon No. 3093[1]

We live in very singular times. The professing church has been flattering itself that, notwithstanding all our divisions with regard to doctrine, we were all right in the main. A false and spurious liberality has been growing up, which has covered us all, so that we have dreamed that all who bore the name of ministers were indeed God's servants; that all who occupied pulpits, of whatever denomination they might be, were entitled to our respect, as being stewards of the mystery of Christ. But, lately, the weeds upon the surface of the stagnant pool have been a little stirred, and we have been enabled to look down into the depths. This is a day of strife, a day of division, a time of war and fighting between professing Christians. God be thanked for it! Far better that it should be so than that the false calm should any longer exert its fatal spell over us. The day is come when we must know who are for the Lord and for his truth, and who are on the side of error. The time is now come when some men, once distinguished among us for the attractiveness of their preaching, must be ranked among those who are opponents of the truth. We did once imagine, in the blindness of our charity, that we all preached one gospel, but now the enmity of the carnal mind has appeared. Carnal churches have chosen to themselves cruel teachers, who have begun to teach strange doctrines, which they mystify by their words, garnish with their eloquence, and try to support by specious logic, apart from simple Scripture.

The time is coming when it shall be openly proved who is on the Lord's side; at this very hour, separations are everywhere taking place. We weep for the cause; we do not weep for the effect. We weep that there should have been such heresies growing up in the midst of the church; but we do not weep when we see those heresies brought out to the day and slaughtered, with what some think remorseless cruelty, but what we believe unflinching justice.

We desire that God may spare to us the men who are still faithful and who will never cease, at the risk of being called bigots, to drag out to the light those who lie against God's gospel, to bring them publicly before the world as opponents of the faith which is in Christ Jesus, whereby we hope to be saved. May God give us courage to stand up for the right!

It is with this in view that I have selected my text, to urge upon you at this time the great duty of standing fast at your post for the truth of God, and the equally great duty of endeavouring, wherever you are, to maintain the right. Do not be carried about by every wind of doctrine. Do not give heed to every schismatic who would lead you aside. Hold fast by the oracles of the Most High. You know what you have been taught and to what end you have been called, and you know the foundation upon which you have been built up. 'Be steadfast, immoveable, always abounding in the work of the Lord' (1 Cor. 15:58). Whatever may happen to denominations, whatever divisions we may live to see, let it be known still that for God and his truth we are prepared to hold our ground, at any expense or at any risk.

Now, first, we have two things mentioned in our text, and then, secondly, we have the relationship which exists between them. The two things are 'the church of the living God' and 'the truth'; the relationship that exists between them is that 'the church of the living God' is 'the pillar and ground of the truth'.

1. The church of God and the truth described

First, then, we have the two things mentioned in our text.

The unity of the church

The first is 'the church of the living God'. Note well its unity. It is not said the *churches* of the living God, but the *church*. God does not have two churches; he has only one. We may be called by different names, and, according to Scripture, we are to be separated, like sheep, into different folds, yet still there is only one flock and one Shepherd. The independence of Scripture is to be practised still. Each church is to be separate, having its bishop and its elders governing in the fear of the Lord, without respect of persons, and without being disturbed by the opinion of any other church.

But though we are separate churches as to our organization, we are really but one church, under one Head, the Lord and Bishop of our souls. There are not two churches any more than there are two Gods; there are not two Lords, there are not two faiths, there are not two baptisms. There is one Lord, there is one faith, there is one baptism; and there is one church holding the one Lord, the one faith, and the one baptism. If any do not hold the truth, we cannot allow that they belong to 'the church of the living God'. It is not for us to adopt the cant phraseology of the present day and say that men may be of the church and yet differ from the truth of God. No, by no means; they are either initiated by the Holy Spirit into God's church, or they are not.

If they are not one with Christ, if they are not washed with Jesus' blood, if they have not received his Spirit, if they have not been humbled to know and believe him to be King in the midst of his own assemblies, if they have not put their trust under the shadow of his wings — whatever they may profess or believe or however they may stand before men — if they do not stand so before God, they do not belong to the one church. And not belonging to that, they cannot belong to Christ.

Though our Lord Jesus Christ has only one church, I believe a part of its members may be found in every denomination, but they do not owe their standing to true fellowship they hold with denominations. There is one great denomination, 'the church of the living God', to which every true believer must belong. Some people allege that the children of God may act on different principles, may believe different doctrines, may be the recipients of different kinds of grace, and that their apprehensions of God and of Christ may be thoroughly diverse. We hold no such opinion. If there is not the vital principle in a man's heart, teaching him the truth as it is in Jesus, he does not belong to the one 'church of the living God'. Thus, then, there is only one church, however divided it may be.

The church as the house of God

You will further observe that the church is called 'the house of God'; and why? Because, first, it had God for its architect; it is not built after man's plan. The tabernacle in the wilderness was framed after the pattern which God gave to Moses on Mount Sinai, and, truly, Christ's church is built after God's own model. It is not moulded according to man's idea; it is not shaped according to his opinion. The will of God, and his will alone, has been followed in the construction of his own house, which is the church.

God has ordained *every* stone, and he has marked where each is to be placed; he planned her walls and her pillars, her foundations and her pinnacles. He has not left anything in the church to the mere caprice of man, but he has comprised every tittle in his own statutes and decrees. He has not given a vague idea for man to develop, but he has made known his own mind in his own Word. There is no designer of the spiritual temple except the infinite Jehovah; there is no architect of the house of the living God but the living God himself.

And not only is he its architect, but he is also its builder. He has not left it for us to dig the stones out of the quarry, or to lay them one upon another. He does the whole work himself. The foundation upon which each living stone is based has been laid long ago, Jesus Christ himself being the chief cornerstone. In his obedience and his sacrifice no creature rendered help. Nor less, as 'the whole building being joined together, grows into a holy temple' (Eph. 2:21), every portion of the structure is the work of God and not the work of man.

To the sacred Trinity we look for the gradual construction of the edifice. In Christ we are 'built together for a habitation of God in the Spirit' (Eph. 2:22). There is never a child of God brought into the church by man's contrivance or man's persuasions; each precious stone is brought there by God, and by God alone.

No child of God is sanctified by man; he is sanctified by the living God. No heir of heaven is fitted into the church by man; God alone puts him into his proper position.

Men at times try to build upon the one foundation with gold, silver, precious stones, wood, hay, and stubble; but God consumes them all, for he will have no building in his church but his own:

> The vast materials all he forms,
> Nor power nor love he spares;
> He guards the building from all harms,
> And all the glory bears.

I have often remarked, when men have been adopting a patent process of building up a church by the revivalist sermons of some crazy-brained preachers, that after the first excitement has subsided, that church has become sickly and fallen into a very sad and grievous state. Those revivalists have often been like locusts in our churches, devouring every green thing, and the revivals they have stimulated have brought us almost to destruction.

God will not have men usurp his prerogative in the building. Though they may with their own hands speedily pile up a mighty structure, yet, like the baseless fabric of a vision, it soon disappears and is gone. In his building, God allows no man to use tool or hammer; he will use men for trowels and hammers, but he will not allow them to make use of themselves or of others. His own hands shall perform it.

Again, it is God's house because God resides there. Wherever the church is, there is God. God is pleased in his mercy and condescension to stoop from the highest heavens to dwell in this lower heaven — the heaven of his church. It is here, among the household of faith, he deigns — let me say it with sacred reverence — to unbend himself, and conduct himself on familiar terms with those around him whom he has adopted into his family. He may be a consuming fire abroad, but when he comes into his own house, he is all mercy, mildness, and love. Abroad he does great works of power; but at home, in his own house, he does great works of grace.

Into this house we have been brought; we trust we live there, and he has manifested himself to us as he does not to the world. A father will reveal himself to his children as he will not to his employees, or to those with whom he mingles in his business. So, in the church, God is pleased to manifest all the greatness of his love, all the marvellous depth of his compassion, and to show himself to his people as he never did to angels, and as he never will do to the unregenerate. It is the house of God because all those who live in it have there an access to their Father, and because they can always find him there, a very present help in time of trouble.

Again, the church is God's house because he provides for it. The household of the church would be starved if God did not provide for it. Does the church need pastors? God gives us pastors after his own heart. Does it need teachers? Then the teachers shall be taught by God. Does it want supplies? He makes for it a feast of 'fat things full of marrow' (Isa. 25:6). Are comforts and luxuries needed? There are the wines on the lees well refined, and at our gates are all manner of pleasant fruits, new and old, which, he says, 'I have laid up for you, my beloved' (S. of S. 7:13).

God always provides for his church, because he is the husband of it, the one who cares for the church and cultivates growth in the church. May God be blessed, he never leaves the church to be provided for by man. We tell you that, in dependence upon God, we will seek to bring you a portion of meat in due season, but we never undertake to provide the meal. The Lord will provide; we are merely his servants, to bring to his people food for their spiritual sustenance.

Beloved, the church is God's own house, and since his Word has taught us that 'If anyone does not provide for his own, and especially for those of his household, he has denied the faith and is worse than an unbeliever' (1 Tim. 5:8), we can never believe that God will leave his house destitute of supplies. No, while he is infinite in goodness, while heaven and earth cannot measure the riches of his estates, while he is the Lord of all flesh and the Monarch of all worlds, we may rely upon it that his house will always be abundantly provided for, and his table bountifully spread.

One more remark here: the church is God's house because in this place God is honoured, and in this place he rules. Among men, it is justly said that 'Without hearts, there is no home.' In the circle of a man's household, he expects to find those 'emulous to please', and if he has children, surely the affection of the little prattlers shall call forth his fond paternal love. However he may be belittled abroad, it is fitting that he should be honoured at home; that is the place where he deserves and commands obedience. There he is master and lord, and every bidding of his should be obeyed.

So, the church is God's house, the abode of his household and his family; therefore, though the world may disobey him, yet his church ever welcomes his presence, rejoices to do his bidding, and listens to his words. In the church, God must always be honoured. Let him speak, and our ears will at once give attention, and our feet will run with swift obedience. 'Behold, as the eyes of servants look to the hand of their masters, as the eyes of a maid to the hand of her mistress, so our eyes look to the LORD our God' (Psalm 123:2), to learn his mind and to do his bidding. May he grant unto you, beloved, this distinguishing sign that you belong to this church, which is the house of God, because by your profession and your practice he is continually honoured!

The truth as God's Word

The second thing mentioned in the text is 'the truth'. What do these words — 'the truth' — mean? Depend upon it, they mean nothing more nor less than is wrapped up with the two covers of the Bible. What is the truth? I might tell you that it is the counsels of heaven revealed on earth, the mind of God made known to men, all the precepts, statutes, and testimonies of the Most High.

I might point you to the person of Christ, his obedience to the law, his death, his resurrection, and his ascension, and tell you that the gospel contained in the writings of the four evangelists is the truth.

Or, once more, I might tell you of the witness of the Holy Spirit, those convictions he brings home to the believer's heart, and the teaching by which he trains up the heirs of glory from the moment of conversion till their final gathering in to the heavenly garner, and say that all the witness of the Holy Spirit is 'the truth'.

But then you might ask me why we should call these the truth. What difference is there between their being true, and their being 'the truth'? I answer, what God says is necessarily true. It is most certainly true, because God has said it. It needs no evidence to establish it, no argument to prove it. Therefore it is so far above evidence and proof that it is really 'the truth'. As your minister, I must assert it, and illustrate it, and preach it as dogmatically as possible, for there can be no appeal against 'the truth'. As disciples, you must believe it, and search it, and explore its depths; but there is no room to doubt, or to reason how much or how little you ought to receive, seeing that it is, without question, 'the truth'.

Note its *importance*. It is called *the* truth. There are many other truths in the world beside God's truth. There is natural truth, the truth of science, the truth of history, and the truth man constantly utters on the evidence of his senses, which we unhesitatingly receive. Yet, though these may be important in some degree, they give way to the all-important truth of God. Now the definite article 'the' is here put before the word 'truth' to teach us that, if everything else we believe to be true should prove true, the whole would sink into insignificance when compared with the importance of the truth of God.

See, then, that you do not underrate the importance of God's truth. I would have you particularly value it, for some think it a matter of comparative indifference, and that, although it is *right* for us to believe all things which God has revealed, yet it is not *important* that we should do so. They suppose that it is of little consequence what sentiments we hold; we may be half right and half wrong and yet be quite as well off; it signifies little what the head believes, so long as the heart is right. Alas! This is a strange infatuation!

The saints of old purified their souls 'in obeying the truth through the Spirit' (1 Peter 1:22). I cannot understand how your hearts can be right while you oppose the truth. Were it only that God has revealed it, you might know that it is of divine importance. It is surely incumbent upon us to believe what he says; we ought to accept what he has set forth as essential to our well-being, our comfort, and our happiness. You may turn a deaf ear to the words of our poets, our philosophers, or our historians; you may even be content to live in ignorance of the laws of your country; but 'See that you do not refuse him who speaks' (Heb. 12:25) to you from heaven. This must be perilous indeed. Mark well, then, the importance of truth, for, in these days, men are apt to esteem it lightly, and for the sake of peace and quietness to lead us to suppose that contrary things can be true.

The truth is not only important, but also *substantial* in its character. The gospel which God has revealed is so essentially *the* truth that there is nothing false, as there is nothing trifling, in it. It is truth unalloyed; it is truth which ought not to be doubted. It is a vile sin to imagine that there can be any fallacy in the utterances of an infallible God. Let everything else we credit be a lie; let all that man has asserted and proved be swept away. God's words are the truth, substantially and really so.

The truth, moreover, is a thing of *unity*. It is not said 'truths', but 'the truth'. God's truth is only one. Have you ever noticed, in the great summary of doctrines, that, as surely as you believe one, you must believe the rest! One doctrine so leans upon the others that, if you deny one, you must deny the rest. Some think that they can believe four out of the five points, and reject the last. It is impossible; God's truths are all joined together like links in a chain. There is but one truth, and one system of truth.

'Then', say some, 'tell us how to discern the truth.' You may judge it by three things: by God, by Christ, and by man — that is, the truth which honours God, the truth which glorifies Christ, and the truth which humbles man. Unless a doctrine exalts God, unless it owns him Monarch of creation and gives him absolute power over his creatures — he the Potter, and ourselves the clay; he moulding the vessels as seems good in his sight, we the vessels that are moulded after his pleasure; God everything, and ourselves nothing — then that doctrine is not the truth.

And unless a doctrine magnifies the atonement — if it asserts that the atonement may fail, that it was made for many who do not benefit by it, that God's purpose in redemption is in any way frustrated — it is not of God, it is of Satan.

If a doctrine teaches that man is possessed of good natural powers, that he is not so fallen as the Bible states, that he can do something to help himself, that his exertions can meet with God's grace halfway, that he can assist a little in the work of salvation, or, at any rate, that he can preserve himself from falling and hold on his way with steadfastness, it is a man-glorifying, God-dishonouring doctrine. Cast it to the winds, for it never came from above. God never intended it to be preached otherwise than as the very foil of blackness against the brightness of his own truth.

2. The relationship between the church and the truth

Now I desire to address you very solemnly on the relationship which exists between the church and the truth: 'the church of the living God, the pillar and ground of the truth'. There is a sense in which the truth is the pillar of the church, for the church is built on the truth. It is on the revealed doctrines of divine grace, such as eternal predestination, immutable affection, covenant security, the responsibility of Christ as the Surety of his people — it is on such doctrines as these that the church is built, and in this sense the truth is the pillar and ground of the church. In another sense, the pillar and ground of the truth is God; he himself maintains his own truth; it is not committed to the hands of mortals to maintain it apart from God.

One of the best proofs of this is that the truth is still preserved in the original purity, after so many hypocritical preachings of it, and so much wresting of it to wrong purposes. While God lives, his truth can never die. There remains the sense in which the church is, as it were, delegated by God to maintain and support the truth. You must understand this then instrumentally: while God is the real pillar and ground of his truth, yet in this world he is pleased to make his children such. Really and effectively it is God who upholds the truth, but instrumentally it is the ministers and elders and members of the church who maintain the truth and hold it firm.

The church as pillar and ground of the truth

In reading this verse, I was pleased with two thoughts that occurred to me: the church is both the pillar and the ground of the truth. Sometimes it is the pillar of the truth, when it preaches the Word, when it administers the ordinances and publicly shows forth the gospel. But sometimes there have been seasons of persecution, when the disciples have not been able to go forth and testify to the world, and then the church becomes a kind of underlying foundation, the ground of the truth.

In the days when Paul stood before Nero, he was like the pillar of the truth; at another time, when he was shut up in the dungeon and could not come forth, he was in his heart like the ground of the truth.

When the church stands boldly out and preaches the Word, it is the pillar of the truth; when it is hidden in the Roman catacombs and cannot proclaim the Saviour's name to the world, still there lives the truth deep in the hearts of believers, and they are then the ground of the truth.

We, beloved, who are of the house of God and of the church of God, are the maintainers and supporters, instrumentally, of God's truth on the earth. Come, then, let me stir you up to do your duty; let me beg of you who love God's truth not to leave it to itself.

Perhaps you imagine that God's truth, being mighty, must prevail without your assistance. It is true — it must and will — but then God has also said that, if you belong to his church, you are to be the pillar and ground of the truth. To leave God's truth to shift for itself is as bad as to leave your own children to provide for themselves. True, the great decrees of destiny shall be carried out, and our Saviour's kingdom shall be established, but it shall be by means. God has honoured you by choosing you to be the maintainers, the testifiers, the pillar and ground of the truth. I will endeavour to arouse you, then, by one or two exhortations, to be faithful to this your solemn duty.

The church's defence of the truth

In the first place, remember how your fathers, in times gone by, defended God's truth, and blush, you cowards, who are afraid to maintain it!

Remember that our Bible is a bloodstained book; the blood of martyrs is on the Bible, the blood of translators and confessors. The pool of holy baptism, in which many of you have been baptized, is a bloodstained pool: many have had to die for the vindication of that baptism which is 'the answer of a good conscience toward God' (1 Peter 3:21). The doctrines which we preach to you are doctrines that have been baptized in blood. Swords have been drawn to slay the confessors of them; and there is not a truth which has not been sealed by them at the stake, or the block, or far away on the lofty mountains, where they have been slain by hundreds. It is only a little duty we have to discharge compared with theirs. They were called to maintain the truth when they had to die for it; you only have to maintain the truth when taunt and jeer, ignominious names and contemptuous epithets are all you have to endure for it.

What! Do you expect easy lives? While some have sailed through seas of blood and have fought to win the prize, are you wearied with a slight skirmish on dry land? What would you do if God should permit persecuting days to overtake you? Oh craven spirits, you would flee away, and disown your profession! Be the pillar and ground of the truth. Let the blood of martyrs, let the voices of confessors, speak to you. Remember how they held fast the truth, how they preserved it and handed it down to us from generation to generation. By their noble example, I urge you, be steadfast and faithful, tread valiantly and firmly in their steps, acquit yourselves like men — like men of God, I implore you!

Will we not have some champions, in these times, who will deal sternly with heresies for the love of the truth — men who will stand like rocks in the centre of the sea, so that, when all others shake, they stand invulnerable and invincible? You who are tossed about by every wind of doctrine, farewell; I do not acknowledge you till God will give you grace to stand firm for his truth, and not to be ashamed of him nor of his words in this evil generation.

The truth revealed to the church

Or again, consider that you have the greatest reason to be the pillar and ground of the truth from the fact that this truth has been of immeasurable service to you. How often has it gladdened your hearts! You were once in darkness, but now you are light in the Lord. Once you had no clear view of that great mystery of godliness, but now God has been pleased to open your eyes, having touched them with spiritual eye-salve, so that in his light you can see light. You are now brought to see that which is revealed, and to believe the doctrines of grace.

Have you not found these things comforting? How often have they supported you in the hour of peril! How often have they checked you when you would have sinned, and guarded you from despair when you were trodden underfoot by the enemy! How often have they nerved your arm for conflict, or moved your foot for journeying! How well accoutred have you been since you believed these things, who were but poor defenceless creatures before!

Will you not, then, maintain the truth, and spread it abroad? Will you blush to own the Word which has brought salvation to your souls, which has rescued you from the thraldom of sin, and introduced you into the liberty with which Christ has made you free? No! I beseech you, by the glorious panoply with which Christ has arrayed you, by his perfect love with which he has covered you, by the crown which he has promised you, by the heaven which he has prepared for you, be faithful to the church of Christ, of which you are members; be still the pillar and ground of the truth.

Reflect once more, as another weighty reason, that you should ever have been led to know the truth at all. Why, you know you did not deserve it. You believe that God has chosen you in his sovereignty, entirely irrespective of your character. You must regard yourself as being the last man in the world that you could ever have thought God would have chosen.

Some of you were sinners against his love and against his law — great, open, and apparent sinners. Others of you were secret transgressors; you sinned against God with a high hand and an outstretched arm, though men did not know it. Many of you were poor sinners involved in the darkness of deceitful doctrine; you had been led astray to believe yourselves saved, whereas you have since found that it was no work of the Spirit, but the mere excitement of your carnal feelings. And now that you, the chief of sinners, rescued by divine grace from death and hell, are brought into his church, will you not, for gratitude's sake, considering what you owe to your Master, defend and maintain his truth at all hazards, in the midst of a gainsaying generation?

The truth a blessing

Then, once more, you are bound to maintain this truth, as you consider the manifold blessings which it will confer upon your fellow creatures when it wins the day. Truth is ever a blessing. Men may hate it, but it is a blessing, and it brings a blessing to their door, though they do not welcome it. They may think it curses them, but the truth is no curse, unless men make it so to themselves.

Nothing can benefit your generation, nothing can ameliorate the morals of mankind, nothing can refine the earth, nothing can wash away its blood, nothing can cleanse its stains, nothing can purge its lusts, nothing can stop its wars and heal its feuds — nothing better, nothing nearly so well, as the maintenance of the truth of God. Therefore, be very bold for it. It is the earth's one hope. Take it away, and that world's brightest star is quenched, and her central sun is dim. Maintain the truth, then, for the world's sake, I urge you.

The truth triumphant

And if encouragement can stir you up to duty, let me remind you that the time is coming when truth shall be triumphant. Soldier of the cross, the hour is coming when the note of victory shall be proclaimed throughout the world! The battlements of the enemy must soon succumb; the swords of the mighty must soon be given up to the Lord of lords. What, soldier of the cross? In the day of victory, would you have it said that you turned your back in the day of battle? Do you not wish to have a share in the conflict, that you may have a share in the victory?

If you are even in the hottest part of the battle, will you flinch and fly? You shall have the brightest part of the victory if you are in the fiercest part of the conflict. Will you turn and lose your laurels? Will you throw away your sword? Shall it be with you as when a standard-bearer faints? No, man, up to arms again, for the victory is certain. Though the conflict is severe, I urge you, on to it again! On, on, you lionhearted men of God, to the battle once more, for you will yet be crowned with immortal glory.

May God, then, grant to us that we may ever stand fast in the fight, as we would stand foremost among the conquerors! Note well those who have already overcome; they are pillars in the house of their God, and they will 'go no more out for ever'. As you mark their white garments, their crowns, their palms, do you not pant to join the triumphant host? I know you do; well, then wrestle hard as they did, and, by divine grace, you also will overcome, and then you will sit down with Jesus on his throne, even as he did overcome, and is set down for ever with his Father upon his throne.

But some will say, 'If we go forth resolved to maintain this truth, we will be called bigots, and we will get very much ill feeling from the world.' Well, if you are afraid of that, I am finished with you; I do not call you kith or kin with me if you are abashed at such trivial rebuffs. If you blush at that, sir, you will never do much for your Master's honour. If you do not know how to stand fast against the world, you will find that the world will stand fast against you.

Did they not call Luther a bigot? Did they not say he was a mere declaimer? Did they not charge him with want of logic, and say he was a man that hurled invectives? But did any of these things move him? No, he persevered, and still spread abroad the savour of his Master's name in every place, till he finished his course with joy as a conqueror.

What sort of a reputation did John Knox[2] have in his day? Were not all manner of accusations heaped upon his head? But what did he say? 'If I be God's servant, and on God's side, I will not start for any one of you.' And now he has this for his epitaph, 'Here lyeth a man who in his life never feared the face of man.' Few of you would merit such an epitaph.

But, says another, 'How am I to know that it is the truth?' That question I answer in this way: if you do not know it is the truth of God, you cannot stand up for it. I am only speaking to men who do know that it is the truth. A true Christian cannot allow that he is in error, for he sees the truth positively written in God's Word. But you tell me that I may err. No, I cannot err when I have God's Word in my lips. People will controvert and will go into endless arguments to show that we are wrong. We cannot be wrong, sirs, we cannot allow ourselves to be even supposed to be wrong when we hold fast by the Scriptures only, for that were to suppose that God's Word could be wrong. Our inferences from Scripture may be wrong, but when we have the genuine Scripture itself, we cannot admit the possibility of our being in error. And unless you are most solemnly convinced that you have the infallible testimony of God in your own consciences and of the truthfulness of his inspired Word, I do not ask you to be defenders of the truth; such defence would be puerile, and I should be more puerile to ask for it.

Another says, 'I don't think it needful to make a noise about doctrine; it does not concern souls much.' Does it not? I believe souls have been instrumentally damned by the thousands by false doctrine. I believe that the universal redemption scheme is doing immense mischief. As Joseph Irons[3] said, 'When men once believe that Jesus Christ died for his elect, they begin questioning, "Did he die for me?", and that stirs them up to seek to know the truth of God. But when they hear that there is salvation for all, they say at once, "Then I may sit still, and fold my arms," and so they are deluded into hell.'

Do you not think that is a soul-deluding doctrine when men are told that they can do all things, and have power to save themselves? They seek to do what they can, and they do a great deal, resting content with a spurious conversion, instead of the conversion which is of God, and not of the will of the creature. I do not believe in all the conversions we hear of as brought about by false doctrine. God forbid that I should! Men who preach false doctrine may be sometimes useful in conversion because they preach some true doctrine, but a false doctrine never converted a soul yet, unless it converted it into worse dangers, and made it ten times more the child of hell than before.

It is foolish for you to cry out that doctrine does not matter. What would you do if it were not for doctrine? How could your soul be saved? How could you enter heaven but for the doctrine of redemption? Aye, and how could you get to glory but for the doctrine of election — the doctrine that you were chosen in Christ Jesus from before the foundation of the world? Say what you like, you will find doctrines far more essential than you ever dreamed of.

Now, how many of my hearers have had any spiritual realization of the preciousness of these things? 'Ah!' cries one, 'I will defend the truth.' Stop, young man! Have you felt in your heart the great doctrine of God's sovereignty? Have you been humbled in the dust to know that God has a right to do with you as he pleases? If not, you cannot defend the doctrine of *divine sovereignty*.

Have you been brought to see the blood of Christ shed specially for you? If not, you cannot defend the doctrine of *particular redemption*, for you do not understand it.

Have you ever felt your own depravity in all its desperate character? If not, you cannot defend the doctrine of *original sin*.

Have you felt that God the Holy Spirit has called you out of darkness into marvellous light? If not, you cannot defend the doctrine of *effectual calling*.

Do you feel in your soul that God has enabled you to persevere up to the moment, and do you have the solemn conviction that you shall hold on your way? If not, you cannot defend *final perseverance*.

I urge you to examine yourselves, and see whether you have these doctrines in your heart. If you have, I will never be much afraid that you will not maintain them, though I think it right sometimes to stir up your pure minds by way of remembrance. As there are too many who would guide your minds into 'the non-doctrine scheme', and feed you with that which is vague and visionary instead of that which is substantial and true, I would the more earnestly exhort you, as for your very lives, to 'Hold fast the pattern of sound words which you have heard from me' (2 Tim. 1:13).

Stand fast, beloved; do not be moved in the evil day; and having done all, stand fast in the Lord. May God grant it for Jesus' sake!

The Word and the Spirit

Chapter 9

Independence of Christianity

. . . The preservation and the triumph of the church are to be accomplished, not by might nor by power, but by the Spirit of God, in order that all the honour might be to God and none of it to man.

9.
Independence of Christianity

Not by might, nor by power, but by my Spirit, says the Lord of hosts — Zech. 4:6

A sermon delivered on Lord's Day morning, 31 August 1857, by C. H. Spurgeon, at the Music Hall, Royal Surrey Gardens. Sermon No. 149

God's first and greatest object is his own glory. There was a time, before all time, when there was no day but the Ancient of Days, when God dwelled alone in the magnificence of his sublime solitude. Whether he should create or not create was a question depending upon the answer to another question — would it be to his honour or not? He determined that he would glorify himself by creating; but beyond all doubt, his motive in creating was his glory. And since that time, he has ever ruled the earth, and even blessed it, with the same object in his infinite mind — his own glory and honour. For God to have a lesser motive would be less than divine.

The highest position to which you or I could attain is to live for God, and the very highest virtue of God is for him to magnify himself in all his greatness as the Infinite and the Eternal. Whatever, then, God permits or does, he does with this one motive: his own glory. And even salvation, costly though it was, and infinitely a gift to us, had for its first object and for its grand result the exaltation of the being and of the attributes of the Supreme Ruler.

Now, as this is true in general of the great acts of God, this is equally true in the minutiae of them. It is true that God has a church, that that church has been redeemed and will be preserved for his glory, and it is equally true that everything that is done to the church, in the church, or for the church, either with the permission or by the power of God, is for God's glory, as well as for the church's well-being.

You will notice, in reading Scripture, that whenever God has blessed the church, he has secured for himself the glory of the blessing, though they have profited by it. Sometimes he has been pleased to redeem his people by might, but then he has so used the might and power that all the glory has come to him, and his head alone has worn the crown.

Did he smite Egypt, and lead forth his people, with a strong hand and outstretched arm? The glory was not to the rod of Moses, but to the almighty power that made the rod so potent.

Did he lead his people through the wilderness, and defend them from their enemies? Again, did he, by teaching the people their dependence upon him, preserve to himself all the glory, so that not even Moses or Aaron among the priests or prophets could share the honour with him?

And tell me, if you will, of slaughtered Anak, and the destruction of the tribes of Canaan; tell me of Israel's possessing the promised land; tell me of Philistines routed and laid in heaps; of Midianites made to fall on one another; tell me of kings and princes who fled swiftly and fell, until the ground was white, like the snow in Salmon.

I will say of every one of these triumphs, 'Sing *to the Lord*, for *he* has triumphed gloriously'; and I will say at the end of every victory, 'Crown *him*, crown *him*, for *he* has done it; and let *his* name be exalted and extolled, world without end.'

Sometimes, however, God chooses not to employ the agency of power. If he chooses to save by might and by power, it is in order that glory may be unto him; and when he says, 'Not by might, nor by power, but by my Spirit, says the Lord', it is still with the same object, and the same desire, that we may be led,

To give to the King of kings renown,
The Lord of lords with glory crown.

God is jealous of his own honour; he will not allow even his church to be delivered in such a way as to honour men more than God. He will take to himself the throne without a rival; he will wear a crown that no head has worn and sway a sceptre that no hand has grasped, for as truly as he is God, the earth will know that he, and he alone, has done it, and unto him will be the glory.

Now, my object will be to glorify God by showing to you, who love the Saviour, that the preservation and the triumph of the church are to be accomplished, not by might, nor by power, but by the Spirit of God, in order that all the honour might be to God and none of it to man. I shall divide my text very simply; it divides itself: first, 'not by might'; secondly, 'nor by power'; thirdly, 'but by my Spirit'.

You may ask whether there is any distinction to be drawn between these two words, 'not by might, nor by power'. I answer, yes. The best Hebrew scholars tell us that the 'might', in the first place, may be translated 'army'. The Septuagint translates it so. It signifies power collectively — the power of a number of men combined together. The second word, 'power', signifies the prowess of a single individual, so that I might paraphrase my text this way: 'Not by the combined might of men labouring to assist each other, nor by the separate might of any single hero, but by my Spirit, says the Lord.' And now you will see the distinction, which is not without a difference.

1. Not by might

To begin then, the preservation and the triumph of the church cannot be accomplished by might — that is, not by might collectively.

The might of human armies

First, let us consider that collective might to represent human armies. We affirm that the church can neither be preserved, nor have its interests promoted, by human armies. We have all thought otherwise in our time, and have foolishly said when a fresh territory was annexed to the British Empire, 'Ah, what a providence! Now a door is opened for the gospel. A Christian power will necessarily encourage Christianity, and, seeing that a Christian power is at the head of the government, it will be likely that the local inhabitants will be induced to search into the authenticity of our revelation, and so great results will follow. Who can tell but that, at the point of the bayonet, the gospel will be carried, and that, by the edge of the true sword of valiant men, Christ's gospel will be proclaimed?' I have said so myself; and now I know I am a fool for my pains, and that Christ's church also has been made to look foolish. The progress of the arms of a Christian nation is not the progress of Christianity, and I hold that the spread of the British Empire, so far from being advantageous to the gospel, has been hostile to it.

You would think that when those who are called Christians had the land, they would favour religion. In India, as I have learned from a clergyman upon whose memory the fact is vividly impressed, a native soldier in a British regiment was converted to God by a missionary. He proposed to be baptized, and become a Christian. He was seen by the chaplain and was received as a Christian. What do you think became of that man? To their everlasting shame, the East India Company[1] stripped him of his regimentals, dismissed him from the service and sent him home, because he had become a Christian! Alas! The policy of greed cannot easily be made to assist the kingdom of Christ.

I would go further. I believe that the help of government would have been far worse than its opposition. If I were to be sent to India tomorrow to preach the gospel, I would feel that when I preached I would be regarded as one of the ruling class — one of the oppressors, it may sometimes be added — and I would not expect my congregation to listen to me as a man speaking to men, a brother to brother, a Christian full of love, but they would hear me, and only cavil at me, because even my white face would give me some appearance of claiming superiority.

Why, our missionaries and our clergymen have assumed a kind of superiority and dignity over the people; they have called themselves clergy, and the people laity, and the result has been that they have weakened their influence. I have thought it right to come among my fellow men, and be a man among men, just one of themselves, their equal and their friend, and they have rallied around me and not refused to love me. And I should not expect to be successful in preaching the gospel, unless I might stand and feel that I am a brother, bone of their bone and flesh of their flesh. If I cannot stand before them in that way, I cannot get at their hearts. Send me, then, to India as one of the dominant ruling race, and you give me a work I cannot accomplish when you tell me to evangelize its inhabitants.

Now just cast your eye upon the wide world. Did you ever hear of a nation under British rule being converted to God? In that day when John Williams[2] fell in Erromanga, Christians wept, but it was a more hopeful day for Erromanga than the day when our missionaries in India first landed there. It is only a people that have been left to themselves, and preached to by men as men, that have been brought to God. For my part, I believe that when an enterprise begins in martyrdom, it is none the less likely to succeed, but when conquerors begin to preach the gospel to those they have conquered, it will not succeed.

God will teach us that it is not by might. All swords that have ever flashed from scabbards have not aided Christ a single grain. Christians' religion must be sustained by love. The great crime of war can never promote the religion of peace. The battle and the garment rolled in blood are not a fitting prelude to 'peace on earth, goodwill to men'. And I do firmly hold that the slaughter of men, that bayonets and swords and guns have never yet been, and never can be, promoters of the gospel. The gospel will proceed without them, but never through them: 'not by might'.

Hush your trumpet, oh war; put away your gaudy trappings and your bloodstained drapery. If you think that the cannon with the cross upon it is really sanctified, and if you imagine that your banner has become holy, you dream of a lie. God does not want you to help his cause: 'It is not by armies, nor by power, but by my Spirit, says the Lord.'

The might of denominations

Now understand this word 'might' in another sense, to signify great corporations, or, as we say, denominations of men. Nowadays, people get strange notions in their head, and they form what they call a denomination. It is all wrong; there never ought to have been any denominations at all, for according to Scripture, every church is independent of every other. There ought to have been as many separate churches as there were separate opinions; but denominations, which are the gathering up of those churches, I take it, ought not to have existed at all. They may do some good, but they do a world of mischief. Now, when a denomination first starts, it is very much opposed. Take, for instance, Methodism: how earnest its first preachers were, how indefatigably they toiled, and how incessantly they were persecuted; yet what a harvest of souls God gave to them! What a great blessing was showered from the cloud that first started at Oxford with those few young men preaching the everlasting gospel! Methodism went on and grew to be a most respectable kind of society, but now the ancient power of Methodism has to a great degree failed. That power, which once seemed to turn the world upside down and set the whole of the churches on fire with a divine light and life, is to a great degree quenched.

The fact is, that just when the corporation began to be the greatest, God said, 'Now then, you have done your work, to a great degree; it shall not be by you any longer, not by might, not by your allied forces. You have said, "Our efforts will cover the earth with the gospel." Now,' says God, 'I will diminish you by thousands. I will take off your membership roll year by year as many as would make another denomination strong; and though you will still exist, you will have to weep and repent with bitterness because of your departed zeal.'

It is just the same with every other denomination. When we Baptists were reckoned to be the poorest lot in the world, and everybody sneered at us, we did far more good than we do now. There was far more pure doctrine and far better preaching than there is at the present time. But we began to be respectable — and just as we began to be respectable we began to lose our power. Every fresh Gothic Baptist chapel was a diminution of simplicity, and every fresh place where the minister became intellectual, as it was called, was just a loss of evangelical might, till now, as a denomination, we are just as low as any other. We need some of our old leaders again, just to preach the word with demonstration and with power, and to overthrow all those grand conventionalisms which have tried to make the Baptist denomination respectable.

I pray to God I may never be called to preach to a much-applauded congregation; it would be a sad and evil day. To be despised, to be spit upon, to be caricatured, and to be jeered is the highest honour that a Christian minister can have; and to be pampered, flattered, and applauded by men is a poor, base thing that is not worth having. If any come here and say, 'They are not a respectable sort of people,' we reply, 'We labour to preach to the poor.' But mark this: whenever a great denomination begins to get too great, God will cut away its horns, and take away its glory, till the world admits, 'It is not by might nor by power.'

The might of many members

And now, I shall give one more application of the word 'might'. It is so with one particular church, just as I have been observing. I tremble for the church of which I am the pastor. I never trembled for it when we were few, when we were earnest in prayer and devout in supplication, when it was a contemptible thing to go into 'that miserable Baptist chapel in Park Street', when we were despised and maligned and slandered. I never trembled for them then; God was blessing the ministry, souls were saved, and we walked together in the fear of the Lord and in love.

But I tremble for it now, now that God has enlarged our borders, and given us to count our members not by tens but by hundreds, now that we can say we are the largest Baptist church in the land. I do tremble now, because now is just the time when we shall begin to say, 'We are a great people', 'We shall do very much', 'We are a great agency', 'The world will look upon us, and we will do a great deal.' If we ever say that, God will say, 'Cursed is he that trusts in man and makes flesh his arm,' and he will hide the light of his countenance from us, so that our mountain that stands firm shall begin to shake.

Oh, churches! Take heed lest you trust in yourselves; take heed lest you say, 'We are a respectable body', 'We are a mighty number', 'We are a potent people'; take heed lest you begin to glory in your own strength; for when that is done, 'Ichabod' (1 Sam. 4:21) will be written on your walls and your glory will depart from you. Remember that he who was with us when we were only a few must be with us now that we are many, or else we must fail; and he who strengthened us when we were merely 'little in Israel' must be with us now that we are like 'the thousands of Manasseh', or else it is all over with us and our day is past. 'Not by might, nor by power, but by my Spirit, says the Lord.'

2. Nor by power

Nor is the preservation of the church accomplished by power, that is, individual strength. You know, beloved, that after all, the greatest works that have been done have been done by the ones. The hundreds do not often do much; the companies never do. It is the units, just the single individuals, that, after all, are the power and the might.

Take any parish in the land where there is a well-regulated society for doing good — it is some young woman or some young man who is the very life of it. Take any church; there are multitudes in it, but it is some two or three that do the work.

Consider the Reformation: there might be many reformers, but there was only one Luther; there might be many teachers, but there was only one Calvin. Look at the preachers of the last age, the mighty preachers who stirred up the churches; they had many fellow-workers, but, after all, it was not Whitefield's friends, nor Wesley's friends, but the men themselves that did it.

Individual effort is, after all, the grand thing. A man alone can do more than a man with fifty men at his heels to fetter him. Committees are very seldom of much use, and bodies and societies sometimes are a loss of strength instead of a gain. It is said that if Noah's ark had had to be built by a company, they would not have laid the keel yet, and it is perhaps true. There is scarcely anything done by a body; it almost always fails, because what is many men's business is just nobody's business at all. It is just the same with religion: the grand things must be done by the ones; the great works of God must be accomplished by individual men.

Look back through ancient history. Who delivered Israel from the Philistines? It was a solitary Samson. Who gathered the people together to rout the Midianites? It was one man, Gideon, who cried, 'the sword of the Lord and of Gideon' (Judg. 7:18). Who was it that smote the enemy? It was one man, Shamgar, with his ox goad, or it was an Elon, who with his dagger put an end to his country's tyrant. Separate men — Davids with their slings and stones — have done more than armies could accomplish.

'But,' says God, 'it is not even by individual might that the gospel is to be spread.' Take 'individual might' in different senses. Sometimes, we may say, it represents learning. We discover here and there certain great and mighty men in learning that can take an unbeliever, strap him on to the dissecting board, and anatomize him in a minute. They are great doctors of divinity; they have achieved the highest titles that can be given them at the universities; they have read the Scriptures thoroughly; they are mighty theologians; they could dispute with John Owen[3] and could entirely take the wind out of the sails of Calvin. They know a great deal, a very great deal; they can write most excellent reviews and are much gifted in philosophical debate.

But did you ever hear, in the course of all your life, of any one of these being blessed by God to lead any great religious movement? Such a thing may have been, but I have forgotten all about it; there may have been such an occurrence, but I do not remember it. This I am sure of: that the apostles of the Lord Jesus Christ had taken no degree, unless it was a good degree in being excellent fishermen. Of this I am certain, that all through the ages God has not often used men of any very great intellectual compass; they have not seemed to be men of profound learning; they have generally been men of determined will and strong principle, but not often of any very high intellectual attainments. Do I, therefore, rail at learning? Oh no, God forbid; the more of that the better. Let men be as wise as they can be, and as learned as they can be, but still the fact remains — and there is no one that can dispute it — that God has often taken the foolish things of this world to confound the wise, in order that men may see it is 'Not by power, but by my Spirit, says the Lord.'

I have the pleasure and happiness of being acquainted with a large number of the most eminent ministers in England. I have walked and talked with them, and spoken to them about the things of the kingdom, and with great pleasure, and I know that they would not think me severe in what I am about to say. Many of those at whose feet we have been prepared to sit as little children, to hear their wisdom, confessed as ministers that when they reviewed their life, they felt that it had been unprofitable. They have been learned, but they would say with Owen, 'I would give up all my talents to preach like Bunyan the tinker.' They have wished that they could have achieved something else besides having attained a name for profound learning and research. My brothers, it is not their fault. They have laboured well and earnestly; I find no fault whatever with them. It is God's supremacy that stamps this upon them and makes them feel the force of it — that it must not be by power, and their very intellectual prowess puts them out of the way — so that they are incapable of being used by God, as a mass at least (though individuals may be), for any very great result in the church, because then it would seem to be by power.

'No, no,' says one. 'If a man is not learned that does not signify much; a man must be eloquent.' That is another mistake. It is not by power of eloquence that souls are saved. I believe every man that preaches the gospel in his heart is eloquent; so I have used a wrong word. I mean, however, that great oratorical powers are very seldom made use of by God for any very great result; not even here is God pleased to let it be seen to be by power. You have heard of the preaching of Whitefield. Did you ever read his sermons? If you did, you would say they were rather contemptible productions. There is nothing in them that I would think could have approached to oratory; it was only the man's earnestness that made him eloquent.

Have you heard any preacher that has been blessed by God to move the multitude? He has been eloquent, for he has spoken earnestly, but as to oratory, there has been none of it. I, for my own part, must eschew every pretension to such a thing. I am certain I never think, when I come into the pulpit, 'How shall I talk to this people in a grand fashion?' I think when I come to preach, 'I have got something to say, I will tell it to them.' How I will tell them does not signify much to me; I shall find the words somehow or other, I daresay, God helping me, but about any of the graces of eloquence, or the words of oratory, I am utterly and quite in the dark, nor do I wish to imitate any who have been masters in that. I believe that the men whom we call eloquent now that they are dead were laughed at in their day as poor bungling speakers. Now that they are buried they are canonized, but in their lives they were abused.

Now, my brothers, I do think that God will generally cast a slur upon fine speaking and grand compositions and so on, in order that he may show that it is not by individual power, but by his Spirit. I could stand in a certain place, and point my finger around in a circle, and I could pause at such a chapel and say, 'There is a man preaching there whose compositions are worthy to be read by the most intellectual of persons, but whose chapel on a Lord's Day morning contains a hundred.' I will point you to another of whose preaching we can say that it was the most faultless oratory to which we ever listened, but his congregation were nearly all asleep. We might point you to another, of whom we could say that there was the most chaste simplicity, the most extraordinary beauty in the compositions he delivered, but there has not been a soul known to be saved in the chapel for years. Now, why is that? I think it is because God says, it is not by power; it shall not be by individual power. And I will say this: that whenever God is pleased to raise up a man by individual power to move the world, or to work any reform, he invariably selects a man whose faults and whose errors are so glaring and apparent to everyone that we are obliged to say, 'I wonder that that man should do it. Surely it must be of God; it could not be of that man.'

No, there are some men who are too great for God's designs; their style is too excellent. If God blessed them, the world — especially the literary world — would cry that it is their talent that God blesses; but God, on the other hand, takes up some rough fellow, truly an earthen vessel, puts his treasure in him, and just shakes the whole world. People cry, 'We do not see how it is, it is not in the man certainly'; the critic takes up his pen, dips it in gall, and writes a most fearful character about the man. The man reads it and says, 'It is just true, and I am glad of it, for if it had not been true, God would not have used me. I glory in my infirmities, because Christ's own power rests on me. If I had not had those infirmities, so much could not have been done, but the very infirmities have insured against men's saying, "It was the man."'

I have often been delighted at some of my opponents. They have sneered at everything in me — from the crown of my head to the sole of my foot; I have been covered with bruises and putrefying sores; every word has been vulgarity; every action has been grotesque; the whole of it has been abominable and blasphemous; and I said, 'Well, that is delightful, now that is good.' And while some persons have said, 'Now we must defend our minister,' I have thought, 'You had better let it alone. It is better that it should be so; for suppose it is true — and most of it is — there is all the more glory to God, for who can deny that the work is done?' And he is a great workman who can use bad tools and yet produce a fine piece of workmanship.

If the conversion of hundreds of souls, if the sobriety of drunkards, if the chastity of prostitutes, if the salvation of men who have been swearers, blasphemers, thieves and vagabonds ever since their youth, is not a grand result, I do not know what is. And if I have been the unwieldy, uncouth, unworthy tool employed in doing it, I bless God, for then you cannot honour me but must give all the glory to him, and to him all the glory belongs. He will have it proved that it is 'Not by might, nor by power, but by my Spirit, says the Lord.'

3. By God's Spirit

And now to conclude lest I weary you. While the progress and advance of the church are to be accomplished neither by the collected might of armies, corporations, or churches, nor by the separate exertions of individuals, neither by the might of learning nor of eloquence, yet both the objects are to be accomplished by the Spirit of God. I was thinking as I was preparing this sermon what a magnificent change would come over the face of Christendom if God were suddenly to pour out his Spirit as he did on the Day of Pentecost. I was then sitting down meditating, and I thought, 'Oh, if God would pour his Spirit upon me, would I not leap from this place where I am now sitting, and on my knees begin to pray as I never did before, and would I not go next Lord's Day to a congregation who would feel a solemn awe about them?' Every word I spoke would strike like arrows from the bow of God, and they themselves would feel that it was 'None other than the house of God, and this is the gate of heaven!' (Gen. 28:17). Thousands would cry out, 'What must I do to be saved?' (Acts 16:30), and go away carrying the divine fire till the whole of the city would be kindled.

And then I pictured to myself what would come over all the churches if they were in the same condition, and all the people received that same Spirit. I had seen the minister from Monday morning till Saturday night doing little or nothing — delivering his weekly lecture, attending one prayer meeting, and thinking himself hard-worked. I saw him suddenly start up from his couch, and go round to all the people from his chapel who were sick, and I observed how he delivered a short address of comfort to the sick, with such holy gravity and such divine simplicity that they lifted their heads from their pillows and began to sing, even in the agonies of death.

I thought I saw others of them girding up their loins and crying, 'What am I doing? Men are perishing, and I am preaching to them only three times a week and am called to the work of the ministry.' I thought I read of all those ministers going into the open air to preach the next Monday night; I thought I saw all of them flying, like angels fly, to and fro across this land.

And then I thought I saw the deacons all full of the Spirit too, and found them, with all their powers, doing everything in the fear of God. I found those who had been lording it over the congregation and acting as rulers no longer seeking to be like Diotrephes; I saw the heavenly influence spread over every mind; I saw the vestries too small for the prayer meetings, and I saw the chapel crowded, and I heard the brothers who year after year had prayed the same monotonous prayer break forth in earnest burning words. I saw the whole assembly melted in tears when the pastor addressed them, and urged them to prayer, and I heard the brothers one by one as they rose up speak like men who had been with Jesus and had learned how to pray. They prayed as if they had heard Christ pray in Gethsemane, that prayer which was such as no man ever prayed.

And then I thought I saw all those members and those deacons and those pastors going out into the world. And, oh, I pictured what preaching there would be, what distributing of tracts, what giving to the needy, what holy living! And then I thought I already heard every house uttering its song of evening praise, and every cottage at its morning worship, sending up its prayer to heaven. I thought I saw inscribed upon every ploughshare, 'Consecrated to God', and on every bell worn by the horses, 'Holiness to the Lord' (Zech. 14:20).

And then I thought I saw the different denominations rushing into each other's arms; I saw the bishop doff his mitre, and clasp his dissenting brother and call him friend, and invite him to preach in his cathedral. And I thought I saw the stiff puritanical dissenter casting away his hatred of conformity, and receiving the Church of England brother to his heart. I thought I saw baptized and unbaptized sitting at one table. I saw Presbyterian, Wesleyan, Independent, and Quaker agreeing in one thing — that Christ crucified was all — and clasping one another's hands. Yes, and then I thought I saw the angels coming down from heaven. And it was not long before I finished my reverie by hearing the shout: 'Hallelujah, hallelujah, hallelujah, the Lord God omnipotent reigns!' It was a reverie, but it will be true some day. By the Spirit of God all this will be accomplished. How and by what means I do not know, but I know the great agency must be the Holy Spirit.

And now, dear friends, let me counsel you. The great thing the church lacks in this time is God's Holy Spirit. You all draw up plans and say, 'Now, if the church were altered a little bit, it would go on better.' You think if there were different ministers, or a different church order, or something different, then all would be well. No, dear friends, it is not there the mistake lies; it is that we need more of the Spirit.

It is as if you saw a railway engine on the track, and it would not go, and they brought along a driver and they said, 'Now, that driver will just do.' They try another and another. One proposes that such and such a wheel should be altered, but still it will not go. Someone then bursts in among those who are conversing and says, 'No, friends, the reason why it will not move is because there is no steam. You have no fire, you have no water in the boiler: that's why it will not go. There may be some faults about it; it may need a bit of paint here and there, but it will go well enough with all those faults if only you get the steam up.'

Now people are saying, 'This must be altered, and that must be altered'; but it would go no better unless God the Spirit were to come to bless us. You may have the same ministers, and they will be a thousand times more useful for God, if God is pleased to bless them. You may have the same deacons; they will be a thousand times more influential than they are now when the Spirit is poured down upon them from on high. That is the church's great lack, and until that need is supplied, we may reform and reform, and still be just the same. We need the Holy Spirit, and then, whatever faults there may be in our organization, they can never materially impede the progress of Christianity, when once the Spirit of the Lord God is in our midst.

But I urge you, be earnest in praying for this. Do you know that there is no reason why I should not have preached so that every soul who heard me was converted, if God the Holy Spirit had been pleased to manifest himself. There is not any solitary shadow of a reason why every soul that has been within the sound of my lips should not have been converted by something said if God the Holy Spirit had been pleased to bless the word.

Now I will repeat, there is not a humble Primitive Methodist, nor a poor insignificant preacher of any sort on earth, who, if he preaches the truth, God the Spirit may not make as useful in conversion as any of the great departed saints who are now before God's throne.

All that we need is the Spirit of God. Dear Christian friends, pray for it; give him no rest until God reveals himself. Do not delay where you are; do not be content to go plodding on in the same old way as you have done; do not be content with the mere round of formalities. Awake, Zion; awake, awake, awake! Put on your strength, Jerusalem, wake up from your slumbers, rise up from your lethargy, and cry to God and say to him, 'Awake, awake! Put on your strength, oh arm of the Lord, as in the ancient days!' Then, when he does it, you will find that it is not by might, nor by power; it is by God's Spirit.

And now I conclude with a very brief address. Sinner, unconverted sinner, you have often tried to save yourself, but you have often failed. You have, by your own power and might, sought to curb your evil passions and licentious desires. With you I lament that all your efforts have been unsuccessful. And I warn you, it will be unsuccessful, for you never can save yourself by your own might. With all the strength you have, you can never regenerate your own soul; you can never cause yourself to be born again. And though the new birth is absolutely necessary, it is absolutely impossible to you, unless God the Spirit does it. I pray for you that God the Spirit may convince you of sin, and if you are already convinced, I urge you to believe in the Lord Jesus Christ, for he has died for you, has washed away your sins; you are forgiven. Believe that, be happy, and go on your way rejoicing, and may God almighty be with you until you die.

The Word and the Spirit

Chapter 10

The Word a sword

It is only because Jesus is not dead that the Word becomes living and effectual and 'sharper than any two-edged sword', for if you leave Christ out of it, you have left out its vitality and power.

10.
The Word a sword

For the Word of God is living and powerful, and sharper than any two-edged sword, piercing even to the division of soul and spirit, and of the joints and marrow, and is a discerner of the thoughts and intents of the heart — Heb. 4:12

A sermon delivered on Thursday evening, 17 May 1887, by C. H. Spurgeon, at the Metropolitan Tabernacle, Newington.
Sermon No. 2010

Those who are fond of a labyrinth of exposition will find a maze perplexing to the last degree if they read the various commentators and expositors upon this verse. This is the question: By the *Word of God*, are we here to understand the incarnate Word, the divine Logos, who was in the beginning with God; or does the passage relate to this inspired book, and to the gospel, which is the kernel of it, as it is set forth in the preaching of the truth in the power of the Holy Spirit?

You shall find Dr John Owen, with a very large number of eminent servants of God, defending the first theory, that the Son of God is doubtless spoken of here, and I confess that they seem to me to defend it with arguments which I should not like to controvert. Much more is to be said on this side of the question than I can bring before you here.

On the other side, we find John Calvin, with an equally grand array of divines, all declaring that it must be the book that is meant, the gospel, the revelation of God in the book. Their interpretation of the passage is not to be set aside, and I feel convinced that they all give as good reasons for their interpretation as those who come to the other conclusion.

Where such doctors differ, I am not inclined to present any interpretation of my own which can be set in competition with theirs, though I may venture to propound one which comprehends them all, and so comes into conflict with none. It is a happy circumstance if we can see a way to agree with all those who did not themselves agree. But I have been greatly instructed by the mere fact that it would be difficult to know whether in this passage the Holy Spirit is speaking of the Christ of God, or the book of God. This shows us a great truth, which we might not otherwise have so clearly noted. How much that can be said of the Lord Jesus may be also said of the inspired volume! How closely are these two allied! How certainly do those who despise the one reject the other! How intimately joined together are the Word made flesh and the Word uttered by inspired men!

It may be most accurate to interpret this passage as relating both to the Word of God incarnate and the Word of God inspired. Weave the two into one thought, for God has joined them together, and you will then see fresh lights and new meanings in the text. The Word of God, namely, this revelation of himself in holy Scripture, is all it is here described to be, because Jesus, the incarnate Word of God, is in it. He does, as it were, incarnate himself as the divine truth in this visible and manifest revelation, and thus it becomes living and powerful, dividing and discerning.

As the Christ reveals God, so this book reveals Christ, and therefore it partakes, as the Word of God, in all the attributes of the incarnate Word. We may say many of the same things of the written Word as of the embodied Word; in fact, they are now so linked together that it would be impossible to divide them. This I like to think of, because there are some nowadays who deny every doctrine of revelation, and yet, certainly, they praise the Christ. The Teacher is spoken of in the most flattering style, and then his teaching is rejected, except so far as it may coincide with the philosophy of the moment. They talk much about Jesus, while they cast away that which is the real Jesus — his gospel and his inspired Word. I believe I correctly describe them when I say that, like Judas, they betray the Son of Man with a kiss. They even go so far as to extol the names of the doctrines, though they use them in a different sense in order that they may deceive. They talk of loyalty to Christ and reverence for the Sermon on the Mount; but they use vain words.

I am charged with sowing suspicion. I do sow it and desire to sow it. Too many Christian people are content to hear anything so long as it is put forth by a clever man in a captivating manner. I want them to test the spirits, whether they are of God, for many false prophets have gone forth into the world. What God has joined together these modern thinkers wilfully put asunder, and separate the revealer from his own revelation.

I believe the Saviour thinks their homage to be more insulting than their scorn would be. Well may he do so, for they bow before him, and say, 'Hail, Master!' while their foot is on the blood of his covenant, and their souls abhor the doctrine of his substitutionary sacrifice. They are crucifying the Lord afresh, and putting him to an open shame, by denying the Lord that bought them, by daring to deride his purchase of his people as a 'mercantile transaction', and I do not know what other blasphemy beside.

Christ and his Word must go together. What is true of the Christ is here predicated both of him and of his Word. Behold, this day the everlasting gospel has Christ within it. He rides in it as in a chariot. He rides in it as, of old, Jehovah 'rode upon a cherub, and flew; and he was seen upon the wings of the wind' (2 Sam. 22:11).

It is only because Jesus is not dead that the Word becomes living and effectual and 'sharper than any two-edged sword', for if you leave Christ out of it, you have left out its vitality and power. As I have told you that we will not have Christ without the Word, so neither will we have the Word without Christ. If you leave Christ out of Scripture, you have left out the essential truth which it is written to declare. Aye, if you leave out of it Christ as a substitute, Christ in his death, Christ in his garments dyed in blood, you have left out of it all that is living and powerful. How often have we reminded you that as concerning the gospel, even as concerning every man, 'the blood is the life' (Deut. 12:23). A bloodless gospel is a lifeless gospel!

A famous picture has been produced that represents our Lord before Pilate. It has deservedly won great attention. A certain excellent newspaper, which brings out for a very cheap price a large number of engravings, has given an engraving of this picture; but, because the painting was too large for the paper to give all of it, they have copied a portion of it. It is interesting to note that they have given us Pilate here, and Caiaphas there, but since there was no room for Jesus upon the sheet, they have left out that part of the design.

When I saw the picture, I thought that it was wonderfully characteristic of a great deal of modern preaching. See Pilate here, Caiaphas there, and the Jews yonder, but the victim, bound and scourged for human sin, is omitted. Possibly, in the case of the publication, the figure of the Christ will appear in the next edition, but even if he should appear in the next sermon of our preachers of the new theology, it will be as a moral example, and not as the substitute for the guilty, the sin-bearer by whose death we are redeemed.

When we hear a sermon with no Christ in it, we hope that he will come out next Sunday. At the same time, the preaching is, so far, spoiled, and the presentation of the gospel is entirely ruined so long as the principal figure is left out. Oh, it is a sad thing to have to stand in any house of prayer and listen to the preaching, and then have to cry, 'They have taken away my Lord, and I do not know where they have laid him' (John 20:13). Rest assured that they have laid him in a tomb. You may be quite certain of that. They have put him away as a dead thing, and to them he is as good as dead. True believer, you may comfort your heart with this recollection, that he will rise again. He cannot be held by the bonds of death in any sense; and, though his own church should bury him and lay the huge lid of the most enormous sarcophagus of heresy upon him, the Redeemer will rise again, and his truth with him, and he and his Word will live and reign together for ever and ever.

Brothers, you will understand that I am going to speak about the Word of God as being, like the Lord Jesus, the revelation of God. This inspired volume is that gospel by which you have received life, unless you have heard it in vain. It is this gospel, with Jesus within it, Jesus working by it, which is said to be living and effectual, and 'Sharper than any two-edged sword, piercing even to the division of soul and spirit, and of joints and marrow, and is a discerner of the thoughts and intents of the heart.'

I shall only talk with you in very simple style: first, concerning the qualities of the Word of God; and, secondly, concerning certain practical lessons which these qualities suggest to us.

1. The qualities of the Word of God

First let me speak concerning the qualities of the word of God.

Living Word

It is 'quick and powerful, and sharper than any two-edged sword' (AV). The Word of God is said to be '*quick*'. I am sorry the translators have used that word, because it is apt to be mistaken as meaning speedy, and that is not the meaning at all. It means 'alive', or 'living'. 'Quick' is the old English word for 'alive', and so we read of the 'quick and dead'. The Word of God is alive. This is a living book. This is a mystery which only living men, quickened by the Spirit of God, will fully comprehend. Take up any other book except the Bible, and there may be a measure of power in it, but there is not that indescribable vitality in it which breathes and speaks and pleads and conquers, as in the case of this sacred volume.

We have in the book market many excellent selections of choice passages from great authors, and in a few instances the persons who have made the extracts have taken pains to place under their quotations from Scripture the name 'David' or 'Jesus', but this is worse than needless. There is a style of majesty about God's Word, and with this majesty a vividness never found elsewhere. No other writing has within it a heavenly life whereby it works miracles and even imparts life to its reader. It is a living and incorruptible seed. It moves, it stirs itself, it lives, it communes with living men as a living Word.

Solomon says concerning it, 'When thou goest, it shall lead thee; when thou sleepest, it shall keep thee; and when thou awakest, it shall talk with thee' (Prov. 6:22, AV). Have you never known what that means? Why, the book has wrestled with me; the book has smitten me; the book has comforted me; the book has smiled on me; the book has frowned on me; the book has clasped my hand; the book has warmed my heart. The book weeps with me, and sings with me; it whispers to me, and it preaches to me; it maps my way, and holds up my goings; it was to me the young man's best companion, and it is still my morning and evening chaplain. It is a live book, all over alive; from its first chapter to its last word it is full of a strange, mystic vitality, which makes it have pre-eminence over every other writing for every living child of God.

See, my brothers, our words, our books, our spoken or our printed words by and by die out. How many books there are which nobody will ever read now because they are out of date! There are many books that I could read profitably when I was a youth, but they would teach me nothing now. There are also certain religious works which I could read with pleasure during the first ten years of my spiritual life, but I should never think of reading them now, any more than I should think of reading the 'a-b ab' and the 'b-a ba' of my childhood. Christian experience causes us to outgrow the works which were the class-books of our youth.

We may outgrow teachers and pastors, but not apostles and prophets. That human system which was once vigorous and influential may grow old, and at length lose all vitality, but the Word of God is always fresh and new and full of force. No wrinkle mars its brow; no trembling is in its foot. Here, in the Old and New Testaments, we have at once the oldest and the newest of books. Homer[1] and Hesiod[2] are infants to the more ancient parts of this venerable volume, and yet the gospel which it contains is as truly new as this morning's newspaper.

I say again that our words come and go: as the trees of the forest multiply their leaves only to cast them off as withered things, so the thoughts and theories of men are but for the season, and then they fade and rot into nothingness. 'The grass withers, and its flower falls away, but the word of the Lord endures for ever' (1 Peter 1:24-25).

It imparts its vitality to its readers. Hence, you will often find, when you converse with revelation, that if you yourself are dead when you begin to read, it does not matter; you will be quickened as you peruse it. You need not bring life to the Scripture; you will draw life from the Scripture. Oftentimes a single verse has made us rise up, as Lazarus came forth at the call of the Lord Jesus. When our soul has been faint and ready to die, a single word applied to the heart by the Spirit of God has aroused us; for it is a quickening as well as a living Word.

I am so glad of this, because at times I feel altogether dead, but the Word of God is not dead. Coming to it, we are like the dead man, who, when he was put into the grave of the prophet, rose again as soon as he touched his bones. Even these bones of the prophets, these words of theirs spoken and written thousands of years ago, will impart life to those who come into contact with them. The Word of God is thus overflowingly alive.

Hence, I may add that it is so alive that you need never be afraid that it will become extinct. They dream that they have put us among the antiquities, those of us who preach the old gospel that our fathers loved! They sneer at the doctrines of the apostles and of the reformers, and declare that believers in them are left high and dry, the relics of an age which has long since ebbed away.

Yes, so they say! But what they say may not after all be true; for the gospel is such a living gospel that, if it were cut into a thousand shreds, every particle of it would live and grow. If it were buried beneath a thousand avalanches of error, it would shake off the incubus and rise from its grave. If it were cast into the midst of fire, it would walk through the flame as it has done many a time, as though it were in its natural element.

The Reformation was largely due to a copy of the Scriptures left in the seclusion of a monastery, and there hidden till Luther came under its influence, and his heart furnished soil for the living seed to grow in. Leave but a single New Testament in a popish community, and the evangelical faith may at any moment come to the front, even though no preacher of it may ever have come that way.

Plants unknown in certain regions have suddenly sprung from the soil; the seeds have been wafted on the winds, carried by birds, or washed ashore by the waves of the sea. So vital are seeds that they live and grow wherever they are borne. Even after lying deep in the soil for centuries, they have germinated at once when the upturning spade has brought them to the surface.

Thus it is with the Word of God. It lives and abides for ever, and in every soil and under all circumstances it is prepared to prove its own life by the energy with which it grows and produces fruit to the glory of God. How vain, as well as wicked, are all attempts to kill the gospel. Those who attempt the crime in any fashion will be forever still beginning and never coming near their end. They will be disappointed in all cases, whether they would slay it with persecution, smother it with worldliness, crush it with error, starve it with neglect, poison it with misrepresentation, or drown it with infidelity.

While God lives, his Word shall live. Let us praise God for that. We have an immortal gospel, incapable of being destroyed, which shall live and shine when yonder lamp of the sun has consumed its scant supply of oil.

Energetic Word

In our text the Word is said to be 'powerful' or 'active'. Perhaps '*energetic*' is the best rendering, or, almost as well, 'effectual'. Holy Scripture is full of power and energy. Oh, the majesty of the Word of God! They charge us with 'bibliolatry'; it is a crime of their own inventing, of which few are guilty. If there should be such things as venial sins, surely an undue reverence of holy Scripture is one of them.

To me the Bible is not God, but it is God's voice, and I do not hear it without awe. What an honour to have it as one's calling, to study, to expound, and to publish this sacred Word! I cannot help feeling that the man who preaches the Word of God is standing, not upon a mere platform, but upon a throne. You may study your sermon, my brother, and you may be a great rhetorician, and be able to deliver it with wonderful fluency and force; but the only power that is effectual for the highest design of preaching is the power which does not lie in your word, nor in my word, but in the Word of God.

Have you ever noticed, when individuals are converted, that they almost always attribute it to some text that was quoted in the sermon? It is God's Word, not our comment on God's Word, which saves souls.

The Word of God is powerful for all sacred ends. How powerful it is to convince men of sin! We have seen the self-righteous turned inside out by the revealed truth of God. Nothing else but the searching Word of God could have brought home to them such unpleasant truth and compelled them to see themselves as in a clear mirror.

How powerful it is for conversion! It comes on board a man, and without asking any leave from him, it just puts its hand on the helm, and turns him round in the opposite direction from that in which he was going before, and the man gladly yields to the irresistible force which influences his understanding and rules his will.

The Word of God is that by which sin is slain and grace is born in the heart. It is the light which brings life with it. How active and energetic it is, when the soul is convinced of sin, in bringing it forth into gospel liberty! We have seen men shut up as in the devil's own dungeon, and we have tried to get them free. We have shaken the bars of iron, but we could not tear them out so as to set the captives at liberty. But the Word of the Lord is a great breaker of bolts and bars. It not only casts down the strongholds of doubt, but it cuts off the head of Giant Despair. No cell or cellar in Doubting Castle[3] can hold a soul in bondage when the Word of God, which is the master key, is once put to its true use, and made to throw back bolts of despondency.

It is living and energetic for encouragement and enlargement. Oh, beloved, what a wonderful power the gospel has to bring us comfort! It brought us to Christ at the first, and it still leads us to look to Christ till we grow like him. God's children are not sanctified by legal methods, but by gracious ones.

The Word of God, the gospel of Christ, is exceedingly powerful in promoting sanctification, and bringing about that wholehearted consecration which is both our duty and our privilege. May the Lord cause his Word to prove its power in us by its making us fruitful unto every good work to do his will! Through the 'washing of water by the Word' (Eph. 5:26) — that is, through the washing by the Word — may we be cleansed every day, and made to walk in white before the Lord, adorning the doctrine of God our Saviour in all things!

The Word of God, then, is quick and powerful in our own personal experience, and we will find it to be so if we use it in labouring to bless our fellow men. Dear brothers, if you seek to do good in this sad world, and want a powerful weapon to work with, stick to the gospel, the living gospel, the old, old gospel. There is a power in it sufficient to meet the sin and death of human nature. All the thoughts of men, though you use them as earnestly as you may, will be like tickling Leviathan[4] with a straw. Nothing can get through the scales of this monster but the Word of God. This is a weapon made of sterner stuff than steel, and it will cut through coats of mail. Nothing can resist it. 'Where the word of a king is, there is power' (Eccles. 8:4).

About the gospel, when spoken with the Holy Spirit sent down from heaven, there is the same omnipotence as there was in the Word of God when in the beginning he spoke to the primeval darkness saying, 'Let there be light' (Gen. 1:3), and there was light. Oh, how we ought to prize and love the revelation of God; not only because it is full of life, but because that life is exceedingly energetic and effectual and operates so powerfully upon the lives and hearts of men.

Sharp and cutting Word

Next, the apostle tells us that this Word is *cutting*. 'Cutting' would be as correct a translation as that of our own version: it is 'more cutting than any two-edged sword'. I suppose the apostle means by the description 'two-edged' that it is all edge. A sword with two edges has no blunt side; it cuts both this way and that.

The revelation of God given to us in holy Scripture is edge all over. It is alive in every part, and in every part keen to cut the conscience and wound the heart. Depend upon it, there is not a superfluous verse in the Bible, nor a chapter which is useless.

Doctors say of certain drugs that they are inert — they have no effect upon the system one way or the other. Now, there is not an inert passage in the Scriptures; every line has its virtues. Have you ever heard of one who heard read, as the lesson for the Lord's Day, that long chapter of names, wherein it is written that each patriarch lived so many hundred years, 'and he died'? Thus it ends the notice of the long life of Methuselah with 'and he died'. The repetition of the words 'and he died' woke the thoughtless hearer to a sense of his mortality, and led to his coming to the Saviour.

I should not wonder that, away there in the Chronicles, among those tough Hebrew names, there have been conversions wrought in cases unknown to us as yet. Anyhow, any bit of holy writ is very dangerous to play with, and many a man has been wounded by the Scriptures when he has been idly or even profanely reading them. Doubters have meant to break the Word to pieces, and it has broken them. Yes, fools have taken up portions, and studied them, on purpose to ridicule them, and they have been sobered and vanquished by that which they repeated in sport.

There was one — a desperate fellow, a member of the Hell-fire Club[5] — who went to hear Mr Whitefield. He stood up at the next meeting of his abominable associates, and he delivered Mr Whitefield's sermon with wonderful accuracy, imitating his very tone and manner. In the middle of his exhortation he converted himself, and came to a sudden pause, sat down broken-hearted, and confessed the power of the gospel. That club was dissolved. That remarkable convert was Mr Thorpe of Bristol, whom God so greatly used afterwards in the salvation of others.

I would rather have you read the Bible to mock at it than not read it at all. I would rather that you came to hear the Word of God out of hatred to it than that you never came at all.

The Word of God is so sharp a thing, so full of cutting power, that you may be bleeding under its wounds before you have seriously suspected the possibility of such a thing. You cannot come near the gospel without its having a measure of influence over you; and, God blessing you, it may cut down and kill your sins when you have no idea that such a work is being done.

Dear friends, have you not found the Word of God to be very cutting, more cutting than a two-edged sword, so that your heart has bled inwardly, and you have been unable to resist the heavenly stroke? I trust that you and I may go on to know more and more of its edge till it has killed us outright, so far as the life of sin is concerned. Oh, to be sacrificed unto God, and his Word to be the sacrificial knife! Oh, that his Word were put to the throat of every sinful tendency, every sinful habit, and every sinful thought! There is no sin-killer like the Word of God. Wherever it comes, it comes as a sword, and inflicts death upon evil. Sometimes when we are praying that we may feel the power of the Word we hardly know what we are praying for.

I saw a venerable brother the other day, and he said to me, 'I remember speaking with you when you were nineteen or twenty years of age, and I never forgot what you said to me. I had been praying with you in the prayer meeting that God would give us the Holy Spirit to the full, and you said to me afterwards, "My dear brother, do you know what you asked God for?" I answered, "Yes." But you very solemnly said to me, "The Holy Spirit is the Spirit of judgement and the Spirit of burning, and few are prepared for the inward conflict which is meant by these two words."'

My good old friend told me that at the time he did not understand what I meant, but thought me a singular youth. 'Ah!' he said, 'I see it now, but it is only by a painful experience that I have come to the full comprehension of it.'

Yes, when Christ comes, he comes not to send peace on the earth, but a sword. That sword begins at home, in our own souls, killing, cutting, hacking, breaking in pieces. Blessed is that man who knows the Word of the Lord by its exceeding sharpness, for it kills nothing but that which ought to be killed. It quickens and gives new life to all that is of God; but the old depraved life which ought to die, it hews in pieces, as Samuel destroyed Agag before the Lord. 'For the word of God is living, and powerful, and sharper than any two-edged sword.'

Piercing Word

I want you to notice next that it has a further quality: it is piercing. While it has an edge like a sword, it has also a point like a rapier, 'Piercing even to the division of soul and spirit.' The difficulty with some men's hearts is to get at them. In fact, there is no spiritually penetrating the heart of any natural man except by this piercing instrument, the Word of God. But the rapier of revelation will go through anything. Even when the 'heart is as fat as grease' (Ps. 119:70), as the psalmist says, yet this Word will pierce it. Into the very marrow of the man the sacred truth will pass, and find him out in a way in which he cannot even find himself out.

As it is with our own hearts, so it is with the hearts of other men. Dear friends, the gospel can find its way anywhere. Men may wrap themselves up in prejudice, but this rapier can find out the joints of their harness; they may resolve not to believe and may feel content in their self-righteousness, but this piercing weapon will find its way. The arrows of the Word of God are sharp in the hearts of the King's enemies, whereby the people fall under him. Let us not be afraid to trust this weapon whenever we are called up to face the adversaries of the Lord Jesus. We can pin them and pierce them and finish them with this.

Discriminating Word

And next, the Word of God is said to be *discriminating*. It divides asunder soul and spirit. Nothing else could do that, for the division is difficult. In a great many ways, writers have tried to describe the difference between soul and spirit, but I question whether they have succeeded. No doubt it is a very admirable definition to say, 'The soul is the life of the natural man, and the spirit the life of the regenerate or spiritual man.'

But it is one thing to define and quite another thing to divide. We will not attempt to solve this metaphysical problem. God's Word comes in, and it shows man the difference between that which is of the soul and that which is of the spirit; that which is of man and that which is of God; that which is of nature and that which is of grace. The Word of God is wonderfully decisive about this.

Oh, how much there is of our religion which is — to quote a spiritual poet — 'the child of nature finely dressed, but not the living child'; it is of the soul, and not of the spirit! The Word of God lays down very straight lines and separates between the natural and the spiritual, the carnal and the divine.

You would think sometimes, from the public prayers and preaching of clergymen, that we were all Christian people, but holy Scripture does not sanction this flattering estimate of our condition. When we are gathered together, the prayers are for us all, and the preaching is for us all, as being all God's people — all born so, or made so by baptism, no question about that!

Yet the Word of God takes quite another way. It talks about the dead and the living; about the repentant and the impenitent; about the believing and the unbelieving; about the blind and the seeing; about those called of God and those who still lie in the arms of the wicked one. It speaks with keen discrimination and separates the precious from the vile.

I believe there is nothing in the world that divides congregations, as they ought to be divided, like the plain preaching of the Word of God.

This is what makes our places of worship to be solemn spots, even as Dr Watts sings:

Up to her courts with joys unknown
The holy tribes repair;
The Son of David holds the throne,
And sits in judgement there

He hears our praises and complaints;
And, while his awful voice
Divides the sinners from the saints,
We tremble and rejoice.

The Word of God is discriminating.

Revealing Word

Once more, the Word of God is marvellously *revealing* to the inner self. It pierces between the joints and marrow, and marrow is not an easy thing to reach. The Word of God gets at the very marrow of our manhood; it lays bare the secret thoughts of the soul. It is 'a discerner of the thoughts and intents of the heart'.

Have you not often, in hearing the Word, wondered how the preacher could so unveil that which you had concealed? He says the very things in the pulpit which you had uttered in your bedroom. Yes, that is one of the marks of the Word of God, that it lays bare a man's inmost secrets; yes, it discovers for him that which he had not even himself perceived. The Christ that is in the Word sees everything. Read the next verse: 'All things are naked and open to the eyes of him to whom we must give account.'

The Word not only lets you see what your thoughts are, but it criticizes your thoughts. The Word of God says of this thought, 'It is vain,' and of that thought, 'It is acceptable;' of this thought, 'It is selfish,' and of that thought, 'It is Christ-like.' It is a judge of the thoughts of men. And the Word of God is such a discerner of the thoughts and intents of the heart that even when men twist about and wind and wander, yet it tracks them. There is nothing so difficult to get at as a man. You may hunt a badger, and run down a fox, but you cannot get at a man — he makes so many twists and turns and has so many hiding places — yet the Word of God will dig him out and seize on him. When the Spirit of God works with the gospel, the man may dodge and twist, but the preaching goes to his heart and conscience, and he is made to feel it and to yield to its force.

Many times, dear brothers, I do not doubt that you have found comfort in the discerning power of the Word. Unkind lips have found great fault with you; you have been trying to do what you could for the Lord, and an enemy has slandered you, and then it has been a delight to remember that the Master discerns your motive. Holy Scripture has made you sure of this by the way in which it understood and commended you. He discerns the true object of your heart and never misinterprets you, and this has inspired you with a firm resolve to be the faithful servant of so just a Lord. No slander will survive the judgement seat of Christ. We are not to be tried by the opinions of men, but by the impartial Word of the Lord, and, therefore, we rest in peace.

2. Practical lessons

I have been all this while over the first part of the discourse. I have only a short time just to show one or two lessons we ought to gather from the qualities of the word of God that I have described.

Revere the Word

The first is this: brothers and sisters, let us greatly revere the Word of God. If it is all that we have said it is, let us read it, study it, prize it, and make it the man of our right hand. And you that are not converted, I urge you to treat the Bible with a holy love and reverence, and read it with the view of finding Christ and his salvation in it. Augustine[6] used to say that the Scriptures are the swaddling-bands of the child Christ Jesus; while you are unrolling the bands I trust you will meet with him.

Draw close to the Word

Next, dear friends, whenever we feel ourselves dead, and especially in prayer, let us get close to the Word, for the Word of God is alive. I do not find that gracious men always pray alike. Who could? When you have nothing to say to your God, let him say something to you. The best private devotion is made up, half of searching Scripture in which God speaks to us, and the other half of prayer and praise, in which we speak to God. When you are dead, turn from your death to that Word which still lives.

Seek the power of the Word

Next, whenever we feel weak in our duties, let us go to the Word of God and the Christ in the Word for power, and this will be the best of power. The power of our natural abilities, the power of our acquired knowledge, the power of our gathered experience — all these may be vanity, but the power which is in the Word will prove effectual. Get up from the cistern of your failing strength to the fountain of omnipotence; for, while the youths shall faint and be weary and the young men shall utterly fall, they that drink here shall run and not be weary, and shall walk and not faint.

Use the Word as a weapon

Next, if as a minister or a worker, you need anything that will cut your hearers to the heart, go to this book for it. I say this because I have known preachers to try to use very cutting words of their own. God save us from that! When our hearers grow hot and our words are apt to be sharp as a razor, let us remember that the wrath of man does not work the righteousness of God. Let us not attempt to carry on Christ's war with the weapons of Satan. There is nothing so cutting as the Word of God. Keep to that.

I believe also that one of the best ways of convincing men of error is not so much to denounce the error as to proclaim the truth more clearly. If a stick is very crooked, and you wish to prove that it is so, get a straight one, and quietly lay it down by its side, and when men look they will surely see the difference.

The Word of God has a very keen edge about it, and all the cutting words you want you had better borrow from it.

And next, the Word of God is very piercing. When we cannot get at people by God's truth, we cannot get at them at all. I have heard of preachers who have thought they ought to adapt themselves a little to certain people, and leave out portions of the truth which might be disagreeable. Brothers, if the Word of God will not pierce, our words will not, you may depend upon that. The Word of God is like the sword of Goliath, which had been laid up in the sanctuary, of which David said, 'There is none like it; give it to me' (1 Sam. 21:9). Why did he like it so well? I think he liked it all the better because it had been laid up in the Holy Place by the priests; that is one thing. But I think he liked it best of all because it had stains of blood upon it — the blood of Goliath.

I like my own sword because it is covered with blood right up to the hilt. The blood of slaughtered sins and errors and prejudices has made it like the sword of Don Rodrigo, 'of a dark and purple tint'. The slain of the Lord by the old gospel have been many. We point to many vanquished by this true Jerusalem blade. They desire me to use a new one. I have not tried it. What have I to do with a weapon which has seen no service? I have proved the sword of the Lord and of Gideon, and I mean to keep to it.

My dear comrades in arms, gird this sword about you, and disdain the wooden weapons with which enemies would delude you! Let us use this blade of steel, well tempered in the fire, against the most obstinate, for they cannot stand against it. They may resist it for a time, but they will have to yield. They had better make preparations for surrender; for if the Lord comes out against them with his own Word, they will have to give in, and cry to him for mercy.

Go to the Word for guidance

Next, if we want to discriminate at any time between the soul and the Spirit, and the joints and marrow, let us go to the Word of God for discrimination. We need to use the Word of God just now upon several subjects. There is, for example, that matter of holiness, upon which one says one thing, and one another. Never mind what they all say; go to the book, for this is the umpire on all questions. Amid the controversies of the day about a thousand subjects, keep to this infallible book, and it will guide you unerringly.

Judge by the Word

And lastly, since this book is meant to be a discerner or critic of the thoughts and intents of the heart, let the book criticize us. When you have issued a new volume from the press — which you do every day, for every day is a new treatise from the press of life — take it to this great critic, and let the Word of God judge it. If the Word of God approves you, you are approved; if the Word of God disapproves you, you are disapproved.

Have friends praised you? They may be your enemies in doing so. Have other observers abused you? They may be wrong or right; let the book decide. A man of one book — if that book is the Bible — is a man, for he is a man of God.

Cling to the living Word, and let the gospel of your fathers, let the gospel of the martyrs, let the gospel of the Reformers, let the gospel of the blood-washed multitude before the throne of God, the gospel of our Lord Jesus Christ, be your gospel, and none but that, and it will save you and make you the means of saving others to the praise of God.

The Word and the Spirit

Endnotes

Endnotes

Foreword. C. H. Spurgeon and his teaching on the Holy Spirit

[1] The bulk of this introduction has appeared already as '"Where the Spirit of God is there is power": an introduction to C. H. Spurgeon's teaching on the Holy Spirit', *Churchman* 106, No. 3 (1992), pp.197-208, used by permission.

[2] C. H. Spurgeon, *Autobiography*, vol. 1, *The Early Years 1834-1859* (London: Banner of Truth Trust, 1962), p.11.

[3] *The Metropolitan Tabernacle Pulpit*, 9:668.

[4] Spurgeon, *The Early Years*, p.387.

[5] Spurgeon, *The Early Years*, p.174.

[6] B. B. Warfield, 'Introductory note' to Abraham Kuyper, *The Work of the Holy Spirit*, trans. Henri de Vries (1900 ed.; repr. Grand Rapids: Wm. B. Eerdmans Publishing Co., 1956), pp.xxxiii, xxviii.

[7] Richard F. Lovelace, *Dynamics of Spiritual Life. An Evangelical Theology of Renewal* (Downers Grove, Illinois: Intervarsity Press, 1979), p.120.

[8] C. H. Spurgeon, 'The Holy Ghost the need of the age', *The Metropolitan Tabernacle Pulpit*, 33:146.

[9] Eric W. Hayden, *Spurgeon on Revival: A Biblical and Theological Approach* (Grand Rapids: Zondervan Publishing House, 1962), p.85.

[10] *The New Park Street Pulpit*, 5:210.

[11] As above.

[12] *The New Park Street Pulpit*, 5:210-12.

[13] *The New Park Street Pulpit*, 5:212.

[14] *The New Park Street Pulpit*, 5:213.

[15] *The New Park Street Pulpit*, 5:215.

[16] C. H. Spurgeon, 'Pentecost', *The Metropolitan Tabernacle Pulpit*, 9:289.

[17] *The Metropolitan Tabernacle Pulpit*, 10:337.

[18] *The Metropolitan Tabernacle Pulpit*, 10:336.

[19] *The Metropolitan Tabernacle Pulpit*, 10:338.

[20] *The Metropolitan Tabernacle Pulpit*, 18:564.

[21] As above.

[22] *The Metropolitan Tabernacle Pulpit*, 16:562.

[23] *The Metropolitan Tabernacle Pulpit*, 16:563.

[24] As above.

[25] For information regarding the Pastors' College, see M. Nicholls, 'Charles Haddon Spurgeon, educationalist', *The Baptist Quarterly*, 31 (1985-1986), pp.384-401; 32 (1987-1988), pp.73-94.

[26] C. H. Spurgeon, 'The Holy Spirit in connection with our ministry', *Lectures to My Students* (London/Edinburgh: Marshall, Morgan & Scott, 1954), pp.186-7.

[27] *Lectures to My Students*, pp.188-9.

[28] *Lectures to My Students*, pp.190.

[29] *Lectures to My Students*, pp.191.

[30] *Lectures to My Students*, pp.192-4.

[31] C. H. Spurgeon, 'The abiding of the Spirit the glory of the church', *The Metropolitan Tabernacle Pulpit*, 32:481ff. My attention was drawn to this text by David K. Straub, 'Charles Haddon Spurgeon and "Spirit-anointed" preaching', unpublished paper, given at the C. H. Spurgeon Pastors' Conference, 10-12 August 1995, William Jewel College, Liberty, Missouri, pp.1-2.

[32] *Lectures to My Students*, p.195.

[33] As above.

[34] Spurgeon, *The Early Years*, pp.531-2.

[35] Spurgeon, *The Early Years*, p.532. For other examples, see Ernest W. Bacon, *Spurgeon: Heir of the Puritans* (London: George Allen & Unwin Ltd., 1967), p.150.

[36] *Lectures to My Students*, p.196.

[37] As above.

[38] *Lectures to My Students*, p.197.

[39] As above.

[40] *Lectures to My Students*, p.199.

[41] *Lectures to My Students*, p.204.

[42] Nicholls, 'Charles Haddon Spurgeon, educationalist', pp.88-9.

[43] For a report on this conference, see 'Impressions of the conference of 1891', *The Sword and the Trowel* (1891), pp.333-7.

[44] C. H. Spurgeon, *The Greatest Fight in the World* (London: Passmore and Alabaster, 1891), p.50.

[45] *Greatest Fight*, p.56.

[46] *Greatest Fight*, p.57.

[47] C. H. Spurgeon, 'Another word concerning the Down-Grade', *The Sword and the Trowel* (1887), p.397.

[48] See also the remarks regarding the personhood of the Holy Spirit by [Robert Shindler], 'Andover theology', *The Sword and the Trowel* (1887), pp.274-80.

[49] Cited Os Guinness, 'Let God be God: church-growth weaknesses to watch', *Tabletalk*, 16, No. 1 (February 1992), p.53.

[50] C. H. Spurgeon, 'The personality of the Holy Ghost', *The New Park Street Pulpit*, 1:29.

[51] *Greatest Fight*, pp.59-62.

[52] *Greatest Fight*, p.64.

[53] *The Letters of Charles Haddon Spurgeon*, collected and collated by Charles Spurgeon, Jr. (Harrisburg, Pennsylvania: Good Books Corporation, 1923), pp.54-5.

Chapter 2. True unity promoted

[1] It has been suggested that the reference is to Hugh MacNeile (1795-1879), who was dean of Ripon.

[2] James Montgomery (1771-1854). Scottish hymnwriter, author of 400 hymns, including 'Hail to the Lord's Anointed', 'Angels from the realms of glory', 'Forever with the Lord'. Editor of the *Sheffield Iris* newspaper for thirty-one years.

[3] Martin Bucer (1491-1551), first of the ordained Reformers to break the celibacy rule and marry. Laboured in Strasbourg as a minister for twenty-five years. Came to England in 1549 at the invitation of Cranmer to aid the English Reformation. Spent the last months of his life as professor of theology at Cambridge University.

[4] Martin Luther (1499-1552), the German Reformer, who ignited the Protestant Reformation by posting his '95 Theses' on the Wittenberg Door.

[5] John Calvin (1509-1564), the French Reformer, commentator and theologian.

[6] A conventicle was an assembly or meeting, a term sometimes applied by way of contempt to the meeting or meeting-houses of Dissenters. Also applied to a secret meeting for religious worship of the Covenanters of Scotland.

[7] Reference to the legal requirement for every inhabitant of a parish to pay a tithe of produce of the land for the support of the local Church of England and its incumbent. Commuted to a cash payment in 1836 and finally abolished in 1936.

[8] John Angell James (1785-1859). Minister of Carr's Lane Chapel, Birmingham, for fifty-four years and author of the Victorian bestseller *The Anxious Inquirer after Salvation*.

[9] William Jay (1769-1853). Minister of Argyle Chapel, Bath, for more than sixty-two years. He preached from the age of 16 to the age of 84, and heard both Wesley and Spurgeon. By the time he was 21 years old he had preached a thousand times. In 1810 Princeton awarded him an honorary doctorate. He was one of the very few Nonconformists to be invited to preach before the Royal family.

[10] Spurgeon was asked to resign from the Evangelical Alliance in response to his sermon against baptismal regeneration. Sermon No. 573, 1864.

[11] Plato (c. 427-347 B.C.), Greek philosopher.

Chapter 3. Pricked in the heart

[1] Llewellyn ap Gruffyd, prince of Wales, d.1281.

[2] John Newton (1725-1807), converted slave trader, preacher and hymnwriter.

Chapter 4. A voice with four messages

[1] Jonathan Edwards (1703-1758). American preacher, theologian, philosopher, writer. Student and then tutor at Yale University. Called to succeed his grandfather Solomon Stoddard at Northampton where he saw many converts during the Great Awakening of 1734-1744. 'Sinners in the hands of an angry God' was preached at Enfield on 8 July 1741 and is perhaps the best known of Edwards' sermons. Ejected from his church after twenty-three years over terms of admission to membership. Became pastor at Stockbridge and missionary to the Housatonic Indians. Elected president of Princeton College, New Jersey, but died within five weeks of that appointment, at age 56, following smallpox vaccination.

[2] George Whitefield (1714-1770). Associate of the Wesleys in the Oxford 'Holy Club', nicknamed 'Methodists'. Ordained in the Church of England, but opposition to his itinerant evangelism by church authorities forced him to begin outdoor preaching, with phenomenal results — thousands were converted in Britain and America. Distanced himself from the Arminianism of the Wesleys in 1743 to help found the Calvinistic Methodist Society.

[3] Crystal Palace, built of glass and iron to a design of Joseph Paxton to house the Great Exhibition of 1851. Erected in Hyde Park, London, then moved to Sydenham 1852-1853; destroyed by fire in 1936.

[4] Cholera during summer months was very commonplace in the capital. In 1854, the year Spurgeon moved to New Park Street Chapel, 6,120 deaths were recorded in just nine weeks.

Chapter 6. The sword of the Spirit

[1] This is just one example of many references by Spurgeon in his sermons to *Pilgrim's Progress*: 'Then said Great-heart to Mr Valiant-for-truth, "You have behaved yourself worthily; let me see your sword." So he showed it to him. When he had taken it in his hand, and looked thereon a while, he said, "Ha, it is a right *Jerusalem blade*." Valiant: "It is so. Let a man have one of these blades, with a hand to wield it, and skill to use it, and he may venture upon an angel with it. He need not fear its holding, if he can but tell how to lay on. Its edge will never blunt. It will cut flesh and bones, and soul and spirit, and all" (Hebrews 4:12).' Spurgeon freely admitted that John Bunyan was his favourite author, and he read *Pilgrim's Progress*, 'that sweetest of all prose poems', at least 100 times, drawing frequently from its imagery for his sermons. He said of Bunyan's copious use of Scripture in his writings, 'Why, this man is a living Bible! Prick him anywhere; his blood is bibline.'

[2] *Bradshaw's Guide*, started in 1839 by George Bradshaw, a Manchester printer, consisting of thirty-two pages of tables covering forty-three English railway lines.

[3] Spurgeon may be referring to his own post-conversion experiences. See chapter eight of C. H. Spurgeon, *Autobiography*, vol. 1, *The Early Years, 1834-1859* (London: Banner of Truth Trust, 1962).

[4] Spurgeon opened a boys' orphanage in 1867 and one for girls in 1880. It is estimated that about 1,600 boys and girls had been helped by the time of Spurgeon's death.

[5] A reference to John Bunyan's *Holy War*.

[6] Isa. 45:22 was the text of the sermon when Spurgeon was converted in the Primitive Methodist Chapel in Artillery Street, Colchester, 6 January 1850.

Chapter 7. Search the Scriptures

[1] Latitudinarianism: a position which shows no preference among varying creeds and forms of worship or which allows latitude in religion (*New Oxford Dictionary of English*, Oxford University Press, 2001).

[2] Spurgeon was born a Congregationalist but came to Baptist convictions as a teenager, and joined the Baptists with parental permission. 'My mother said to me one day, "Ah, Charles! I often prayed the Lord to make you a Christian, but I never asked that you might become a Baptist."' *Autobiography*, vol. 1, *The Early Years, 1834-1859* (London: Banner of Truth Trust, 1962), p.45.

[3] James Durham (1622-1658), Scottish minister who first served as a captain in the army during the Civil War before going into the ministry.

[4] Probably Andrew Gray (1633-1656), ordained at age 21 to the pastorate of Outer High Church in Glasgow, where his eloquent rhetorical preaching attracted huge crowds, many of whom, because of lack of room, had to be directed to other churches such as James Durham's. He died after only three years in the ministry.

[5] Titus Livius (59 B.C.- A.D. 17), author of the *History of Rome* in 142 volumes; only thirty-five volumes survive.

[6] Quintus Horatius Flaccus (65-68 B.C.), Roman lyric poet and satirist.

[7] Robert Murray McCheyne (1813-1843), minister of St Peter's Church, Dundee, from 1836 and member of a committee sent to Palestine to investigate possible mission to the Jews.

[8] Harriet Beecher Stowe (1811-1896), U.S. author of the famous anti-slavery novel *Uncle Tom's Cabin*.

[9] David Livingstone (1813-1873), Scottish doctor, missionary, and explorer in central and southern Africa who discovered Victoria Falls in 1855.

[10] Spurgeon was committed to the doctrines of grace and their practical outworking.

Chapter 8. The church of God and the truth of God

[1] This sermon was originally preached in the context of a particular controversy of Spurgeon's day, and an abridged version appears here. More information is contained in vol. 1 of Spurgeon's autobiography, *The Early Years*, pp. 471-95.

[2] John Knox (1514-1572), the great Scottish Reformer, who lived ten years in voluntary exile in Germany, France and Switzerland. He spent time at Geneva with John Calvin where he learned Presbyterian-Calvinistic doctrines. He returned to Scotland in 1559 to assist the Reformation in Scotland, was arrested and tried for treason at the instigation of the Catholic Queen, Mary Stuart, but was acquitted and continued his preaching and counselling ministry at Edinburgh and St Andrews with great influence until his death.

[3] Joseph Irons, minister in Camberwell noted for publishing a weekly sermon from 4 June 1848 until his death in 1852.

Chapter 9. Independence of Christianity

[1] East India Company, chartered by Elizabeth I in 1600 for trade with the East. Activities largely confined to India after 1623 where it thrived on textile exports. After Clive's victories over French rivals in the 1750s, he became virtual ruler of India. The British government assumed direct control after the Indian mutiny in 1858. Company dissolved in 1874.

[2] John Williams (1796-1839), sent by the London Missionary Society (LMS) to Polynesia. Murdered in the New Hebrides Islands after many years of successful church planting in many islands. The author of *A Narrative of Missionary Enterprises in the South Sea Islands* and the translation of the New Testament in the Rarotongan language.

[3] John Owen (1616-1683), important Puritan divine of Independent views. Asked to preach before Parliament the day following the execution of Charles I. Firm friend and chaplain of Oliver Cromwell, serving in the armies in Ireland and Scotland during 1649-1651. Appointed dean of Christ Church College Oxford by Parliament, and in 1654 vice chancellor of the university. After the Restoration of the monarchy in 1660 he was tolerated and even treated with respect and permitted to continue preaching. In 1673 he became minister of a large congregation in Leadenhall Street, London. Authored a vast number of theological works and a long commentary on the book of Hebrews; one of Britain's most important theologians to date.

Chapter 10. The Word a sword

[1] Homer (eighth-century B.C.), Greek epic poet regarded as author of the *Illiad* and the *Odyssey*.

[2] Hesiod (eighth-century B.C.), Greek poet and author of the didactic poem *Works and Days*, on farming.

[3] Both Giant Despair and Doubting Castle are references to John Bunyan's *Pilgrim's Progress*.

[4] The precise definition of leviathan is open to some speculation, but a number of suggested identifications have been made. The word occurs in five Old Testament passages and is used to describe the crocodile (Job 41), a dragon (Job 3:8), and a sea monster (Ps. 104:26). It also is used symbolically of Pharoah (Ps. 74:14), Assyria, and Babylon (Isa. 27:1).

[5] The Hell-fire Club was an eighteenth-century gentlemen's gathering with a dubious reputation.

[6] Augustine (354-430), Bishop of Hippo in North Africa and one of the most important theologians of the Christian church. Converted from a dissolute lifestyle at the age of 33 in Milan upon reading Romans 13:13-14. The Reformers placed his writings second only to the Bible in importance.